EATING FOR ENGLAND

Photography by Tony Harris and Dave Rogers/Allsport

Contents:

Front cover Lawrence Dallaglio, inside cover Phil Greening, back cover Jason Leonard

Freddie, Jayne, Joe, Clive and Jess Woodward

Foreword by Clive Woodward

This is the third project for the England rugby team in support of The Sporting Chance Appeal. In the first year we sold over 1,000 signed England shirts and raised more than £100,000. The second year was our naked calendar which raised in excess of £250,000. This exciting book has come to fruition in 4 stages:

1 I would like to thank our opposition from the southern hemisphere! My first four games as the England coach were against Australia, New Zealand, South Africa and again New Zealand. All within four weeks in the autumn of 1997. We drew two and lost two. It was blatantly obvious to me that we were behind those three teams in every aspect that is a prerequisite in creating a high performance team.

One of the key elements missing was again obvious – we were nowhere near as fit or powerful as a team as our Southern Hemisphere rivals. The reasons for this were many, but they were irrelevant to me. I had to act to rectify this for the England team. It was my first priority.

2 I persuaded the RFU to allow me to employ a full-time expert covering fitness and nutrition. Dave Reddin, who had been working with me during the previous year, joined me full time in January 1998. Three years later England are arguably the fittest and most powerful team in world rugby. Dave Reddin is now regarded as a world authority in the field of fitness and power.

3 Shortly after his appointment Dave made it abundantly clear to me that we needed to work with a company with expertise in food and nutrition. Again the RFU sanctioned my request for a huge investment for our elite players. Dave chose the Centre for Nutritional Medicine (CNM) and the two people we have worked closely with are Roz Kadir and Dr Adam Carey, since the inception of the programme in 1998.

The elite England players follow the advice and guidance given by Dave, Adam and Roz. The fitness and power of the team today is testament to the work of these 3 outstanding people.

I would also like to commend the England players for their courageous efforts to reach such high standards of fitness through their hard work and many hours spent in the gym.

4 My wife, Jayne, came to me with an idea of building upon all of this by working with Anne Menzies, a leading creator of recipes and fellow disciple of healthy, wholesome eating. Anne has subsequently worked with Dave and CMN and built on and created new recipes based upon their lifestyle principles that will not only benefit the England Team but as part of this book benefit the whole nation – to me the icing on the cake.

We have produced this book to enable you to share in the enjoyment of good food and healthy eating. This book and your support of us in buying it, enables us to help our disabled friends in sport. No-one involved in creating this book has charged for their services and all proceeds go to The Sporting Chance Appeal. The concept of an able-bodied team supporting disabled athletes has always been close to my heart.

Finally I would like to express my gratitude on behalf of the England Team to everyone involved in putting this book together.

Introduction by Anne Menzies

Anne Menzies with Lawrence Dallaglio

If I eat from this book, will I look like a rugby player? The only difference between a top rugby player and an ordinary person is the word 'and'. Most of us are advised to eat 'quality not quantity'. But a rugby player eats 'quality and quantity'. That is the difference. Eating from this book is all about quality, just how much you eat is up to you.

Inside each England rugby player is a real person, its just that he needs significantly more food than the rest of us. To perform optimally he eats a quality regime of nutrient rich foods which are low in saturated fat. He correctly mixes a combination of fast and slow releasing carbohydrates which are balanced according to output during the course of the day. A high protein intake is necessary to build muscle and carry out structural repair. To develop the physique of a top rugby player not only demands the correct genetic make-up but stringent mental, physical and dietary discipline.

The rest of us however, can use the same nutritional principles to our advantage and this book tells you how. Eating for England recipes have been developed for optimum performance – whoever you are, because in essence we all work in the same way.

Eating for England recipes are for everybody! The England team reflect the population at large. There are some who love to cook and others who like to leave it to their partners or wives. Some have very conservative tastes and others are adventurous. But they all like to eat together with their friends and families, so the food that they eat needs to be enjoyed by everyone. Many have children in whom they too wish to nourish excellence. These recipes bring together all of their tastes.

Time is important to us all. We feel that if our recipes place too many demands then it makes it easy to revert to bad habits. Everything can be prepared in under 30 minutes - most of the soups take less than 15 minutes. And if you eat half and freeze half, that really does reduce the time you spend in the kitchen. All recipes are simple and under ten ingredients which can be easily sourced from any supermarket. The only extra piece of equipment you need is a blender!

Apart from the odd dab of rugby humour, there is lots in here that you will not find in any other recipe book. There are formulae for creating your own recipes. The Great Green Salad gives the basic proportions to create your own balanced salad and the freedom to come up with any one of 2,000 choices! There are a variety of delicious Power Drinks which perform specific functions and can be made in minutes. Delicious snacks and meals deliver high performance nutrition.

This is a recipe book of empowerment. We deliver what you need to know to help your body do its best. We translate our dietary knowledge into delicious and easy recipes as well as providing the tools to be creative for yourself.
Ultimately, however, the choice comes from you.

Dave Reddin National Fitness Adviser - Rugby Football Union

Dave Reddin with Karl Edmunds (Pennyhill Park)

As part of my job as National Fitness Adviser, I am constantly looking for new ideas and approaches that will give the players and the team an edge.

During 1997 and 1998 I had been looking closely at our nutrition programme, and decided that we could do better. Most nutritionists at that time were preaching that all sports people should follow the same basic diet – high carbohydrate (with no reference to what type), relatively low protein, and low fat.

I knew from my own studies and experience that this approach worked well for endurance athletes, and also up to a point for rugby players. However, it was not an edge – everyone did it this way.

It was through Mike Yates, the fitness coach at Saracens RFC that I first met Dr Adam Carey and Roz Kadir at the Centre for Nutritional Medicine (CNM). After meeting them, I was convinced that they offered something different. In short, a more precise and to my mind much more logical use of nutrition as an edge to performance.

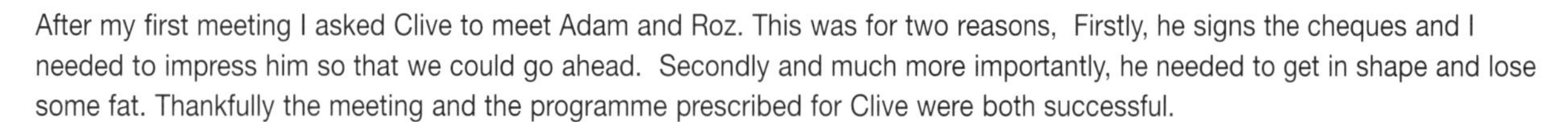

After my first meeting I asked Clive to meet Adam and Roz. This was for two reasons, Firstly, he signs the cheques and I needed to impress him so that we could go ahead. Secondly and much more importantly, he needed to get in shape and lose some fat. Thankfully the meeting and the programme prescribed for Clive were both successful.

We started using our new approach to nutrition at our World Cup training camp in Australia. The impact on the players was fantastic. As you might expect, not all the players are angels when it comes to food. However, most now realise it is not possible to train, play and recover from international rugby, unless your nutrition is good. For elite sports people nutrition provides the platform for improvement. As I am fond of saying to our players, ' You don't put diesel in a Ferrari!'

While not everyone reading this book will be a Ferrari, what you eat does have an enormous impact on how you feel, look and perform in every walk of life.

The basic principles of the nutritional approach we use with the England team are contained in the fabulous recipes in this book. Following the advice here may not turn you into Phil Greening or Martin Johnson, but it will help you maintain higher energy levels, feel more alert, be healthier as a result of a better nutrient intake, and if used correctly with appropriately planned training, control your weight.

I am delighted to have been involved in the writing of this book. It's great to be able to share with you some of the knowledge we use with our top players. What makes it even more satisfying is that in buying this book you are helping us to help some of the amazing people at Stoke Mandeville.

Roz Kadir Centre for Nutritional Medicine

Roz Kadir with Dr Adam Carey

Dr Adam Carey and I started to look after some players at Saracens RFC back in 1998. Fortunately for us, one of these individuals was Kyran Bracken who was impressed with the benefits he felt he gained from sorting out his nutrition.

As a result, he spoke to Dave Reddin, the team fitness adviser who, once he had checked us out suggested that Clive come and meet us. We spent a very interesting Saturday morning in our clinic in Harley Street explaining how we worked. Having convinced both Dave and Clive that we were worth trying, we were sent Neil Back as our first player.

We were very impressed with Neil's extraordinary devotion and commitment to being the best. I remember his words vividly 'if you tell me that eating tree bark will improve my game, then I'll do it'. Fortunately for him, this was not necessary.

Neil wrote about his experiences in his autobiography describing how we ran various tests including sending a sample of hair to the lab to check for toxic metals, and giving him some scales to enable him to weigh and record all his food intake for a week. This gives us a fairly accurate picture of the mixture of foods players are eating before we start work. We made some suggestions as to how he could start improving his nutritional intake and encouraged him to give up some of his favourite foods. Over a period of time he gained about 5kgs of muscle and reduced his body fat by 4kgs.

The rest you might say is history. Since then we have worked with many players and have found that they all feel the benefits of cleaning up their diets and eating foods in the proportions and quantities recommended to them. Those of you who have been following the squad over the past few years will probably have noticed how the combination of improved eating, excellent training advice and (one hopes) adequate rest has paid off.

Even Clive has allowed us to put him through his paces enabling him to shed a few pounds of fat acquired during frequent stops at petrol stations. By choosing tasty but better quality snacks than crisps and chocolate bars, and increasing his protein intake while decreasing carbohydrates, Clive managed to reduce his body fat. He also noticed an improvement in mental acuity which was a very valuable benefit for a man with such a heavy work schedule.

Adam and I have had enormous fun working with the England players and their management team. It has not always been easy but the rewards have been great. It is very much a team effort, and having the support and backing of Clive and Dave has enabled us to provide the sort of support and education that have enabled the boys to make so many improvements.

We look forward to working with many more players in the future.

Some important nutritional inside knowledge.

PROTEINS

These are found in fish, poultry, meat, eggs and dairy products. Most dairy products are not the best source of protein as they are usually high in saturated fats. Fish is low in saturates but high in the healthier unsaturated fats (omega 3) of which most people do not get enough. Vegetarian sources include tofu and Quorn. Combining grains and beans is another way to obtain a full range of the nutrients that make up proteins. Examples such as beans on wholegrain toast, brown rice and lentils, hummus with chickpeas and sesame seeds are all good choices. Protein is an essential part of each meal and should be included to help control blood sugar levels and aid appetite control. We do advise higher than average intakes of protein for rugby players. This has been shown to produce favourable changes in muscle mass. According to a report from The First International Scientific Congress on Nutrition and Athletic Performance held in Edmonton, Canada, in August 2001. There seems to be little lasting harm that can be done by high protein intakes and this is in sharp contrast to the chronic debility that can be expected in later life from insufficient nutrient intakes to support the development of optimal bone density at critical stages of life. New work on this theme will provide us with specific amino acid formulae for bone growth, and deposition of muscle after resistance training, as well as repair after injury and intensive training.

CARBOHYDRATES

Many people think these are only found in grains, when in fact vegetables and fruit are the best natural sources available. Unrefined carbohydrates are those that have not been processed. They require a lot of digestion and provide a steady supply of energy, and include all vegetables, some wholegrains and fruit. Refined carbohydrates include most breakfast cereals, white bread, white pasta, biscuits and cakes.

Generally we rely too heavily on grains and these may cause disturbances to gut function. It is not uncommon for individuals to consume wheat several times a day in cereals, biscuits, sandwiches, pasta and pizza. In so doing we can become sensitive to them. All the more reason, therefore to have lots of variety. You may find you feel better for not eating wheat on a daily basis. Most supermarkets stock wheat-free pastas and breads.

FATS

It is commonly believed that if a food is labelled as 'low fat' it must be healthier. Breakfast cereals are a perfect example of this. They are marketed as 'fortified' and low or almost fat free, but they all contain vast amounts of refined carbohydrates. For example, 100 grams of 'Frosties' contains 41.9grams of sugar. Sugar is readily converted and stored as fat in the body so do learn to read labels. Look at the list of ingredients to see how up in the order sugar appears. Generally if it is one of the first three ingredients there will be a lot.

Not all fats are bad. In fact few people get anywhere near the required amount of good oils needed for prime health. We need them for healthy skin and hair, to absorb fat soluble vitamins (A, D, E and K) for immunity, hormone synthesis, health of blood vessels, muscle reflexes and many other essential processes. One of their most important functions is to reduce inflammation so they are an important part of a rugby player's intake. They also help reduce inflammation associated with arthritic problems. Good oils are found in fish, particularly those with teeth; flax or walnut oil and raw unsalted nuts and seeds.

Saturated fats, most of which come from animal produce are best kept to a minimum, although a little organic butter is fine and often preferable to some of the processed spreads available in the shops.

GLYCAEMIC INDEX – WHAT DOES IT MEAN?

The story

Never before have there been as many low-fat or fat-free products available, yet Western society is more obese than ever. One key issue is that many of these low-fat foods are high in sugars. Keeping fat intake low while also controlling carbohydrates in the form of sugars is the secret of sustainable reduction in body fat.

A diet that is high in sugar and refined carbohydrates will lead to an increase in body fat. After a meal, the gut breaks down carbohydrates into glucose, the glucose is absorbed from the gut and it is burnt for energy or stored. If the carbohydrates you eat require little digestion, glucose becomes rapidly available in the gut and is absorbed quickly. The level of glucose in the blood is controlled by insulin, which acts to ensure that blood glucose levels do not rise above the normal range. It moves glucose from the blood into cells. The faster blood glucose rises, the more insulin is produced. Poor blood glucose control occurs for a number of reasons. The most common and most important reasons are consumption of rapidly absorbed sugars, over stimulation of the pancreas and nutrient deficiencies, which reduce the impact of insulin on the body.

- Take care to match your input (food eaten) with output (energy burnt) by adjusting portion sizes to match your level of physical activity.
- Remember that reducing food intake will lead to muscle loss rather than fat loss. Choose foods that break down slowly and so supply a steady stream of energy instead of being stored as fat.
- Experiment to learn what quantity of carbohydrates you need to fulfil your energy requirements. Spread it throughout the day rather than having a large serving at night.

The Glycaemic Index (GI) is a number that is only given to carbohydrate foods to show how fast blood glucose will rise. The higher the GI the more disruption to blood glucose is caused. The lower the GI the slower the food is broken down. We can therefore use the GI as a guide to which ones to eat. Choose low GI foods except after sustained exercise, when the higher ones will quickly replenish depleted glycogen (energy) stores.

EAT LESS (unless within an hour after exercise)	EAT MORE Sugars
Sugars	**Sugars**
Glucose (100)	Fructose (20)
Honey (87)	
Vegetables	**Vegetables**
Parsnips (98)	Soybeans (15)
Carrots (90)	Kidney Beans (30)
White Potatoes (70)	Lentils (25)
	Sweet Potatoes (48)
Fruit	**Fruit**
Bananas (65)	Apples (36)
Raisins (68)	Oranges (40)
Grains	**Grains**
White pasta (56)	Wholewheat pasta (40)
Cornflakes (85)	Oats (48)
White Rice (70)	Brown rice (60)
White Bread (76)	Brown bread (64)
High GI = > 70, Low GI = < 50.	

The effect of a meal on blood glucose will be less when the meal includes protein, unrefined carbohydrates and fibre. This is one of the reasons why we recommend that protein should feature in all meals and snacks.

More detailed information on this subject can be found on the internet and in bookshops.

IMPORTANT PRINCIPLES

1. HYDRATION

Water is the most important nutrient. Few people come even close to the required amount. Thirst is actually a poor indicator of hydration. By the time you reach this stage you are already dehydrated. The minimum amount required for an active normal sized adult is two to three litres a day. This figure rises if you exercise or if the weather is hot. If you find it hard to consume adequate amounts use fresh juice as you might use squash and dilute it. If your urine is dark and strong smelling you are dehydrated - It should be pale and clear.

2. VARIETY

By choosing a wide variety of foods with a good mix of proteins, carbohydrates and good fats you increase your likelihood of consuming the full range of nutrients, vitamins and minerals you require.

3. EAT FIVE OR SIX SMALL MEALS.

Most people experience energy dips at certain times of the day, particularly mid-afternoon. The way to avoid this is to reduce fluctuations in blood sugar levels by having three small meals and two snacks a day. Many people already do this but their snack choices may not be appropriate. Replace biscuits and crisps with a piece of fruit and a handful of nuts, or a couple of oatcakes with cottage cheese or other protein you like.

4. ANTI-NUTRIENTS

Coffee, tea, other caffeinated drinks such as colas, alcohol and tobacco are anti-nutrients that can have a toxic effect on the body. They can also increase your requirements for vital nutrients. Alcohol causes low blood sugar levels and dehydration. Government recommendations suggest that women should consume no more than 14 units per week and men 21 but less would be better. Coffee and tea dehydrate as you excrete more fluid than you drink. Smoking is sporting suicide and has nothing to promote it.

5. FRUIT AND VEGETABLES

Most people understand this to mean eat 5 portions of fruit a day. Vegetables generally contain more fibre and certainly less sugar. Fruits that are grown close to the equator are more sugary so bear this in mind if trying to reduce body fat. The best rule to follow is to have five portions of vegetables a day, and some fruit, ideally not more than two pieces.

6. FIBRE

Fibre is much more than a bowl of bran. Roughage or fibre from plants is also an excellent and more natural source. Fibre prevents constipation and reduces the risk of bowel cancer. You should aim to consume five portions of vegetables a day as this will get you close to the required 40g necessary for good health. Most people struggle to reach half of this. It is of particular importance if you are on a high protein diet.

7. ENERGY FROM EXERCISE

Great eating habits are only part of the picture. The human body is designed to be used. Inactivity is a sure-fire route to increased risk of heart disease, diabetes and other degenerative disorders. Today's habits of driving everywhere, sitting at a desk and using a remote control to change television channels are a formula for loss of energy and well-being.

Exercise does not have to be boring or only taken in a gym. Park your car some distance from the office or use the stairs instead of the lift. Find an activity you enjoy as you are more likely to stick with it, particularly if you can find a friend to join you. Housework is a great all body workout. By using your muscles, you can burn fat, feel better and eat more!

This book is about good nutrition, not about weight loss or special diets. The word "diet" conjures up thoughts of weight loss plans that can lead to obsession. Good nutrition is easy and straightforward, not rocket science. Understanding how it works should enable you to "eat to live", not " live to eat". Where possible, eat organic, free-range foods. Home produced organic is best when you can find it. In spite of the arguments that rage in the press as to whether it is worth it, our advice is that it is. It will contain fewer pesticides and have higher levels of vitamins and minerals as it is grown on soil that is richer in nutrients. Intensive farming must inevitably lead to a reduction in the nutritional value of foods. If finances are an issue give preference to foods that contain fat as these are more likely to contain higher residues than proteins and carbohydrates as they are preferentially stored in fat.

To look like Martin Johnson, you not only need a lot of the right food, you also need the right genetics, the right mental attitude and the right training. This book gives you some help with one important part of a rugby players life – his food. The recipes have been designed with your enjoyment in mind and therefore do not necessarily follow the very strict protocols which would be required for the nutritional needs of an elite athlete. Everyone can enjoy the benefits of the principles in this book – that is the easy bit. Looking and playing like Martin Johnson is a lot harder! Many women worry that by weight training and eating more protein they will "bulk up" too much. This is very unlikely as men tend to build muscle more easily due to their differing hormones. Testosterone is known to drive muscle growth and women have much less than men. Certainly, in CNM's experience, most people find that by reducing their carbohydrate intake (providing this is appropriate) and increasing their protein intake they can reduce their body fat favourably.

Good health consists of three things – a third rest, a third exercise and a third nutrition. Compromise on one and you may not reap the benefit of the others. Do not be too fundamentalist about making nutritional changes, so start by improving breakfast and then make snacks better quality. Observe the 80/20 rule. If you get it right 80% of the time, the other 20% will not matter so much. By having a day off to enjoy a favourite food you may find it easier to avoid these foods at other times. Just ensure that you do not undo all the good work of the week.

scrum-y soups

Soup makes a great start to a meal, a snack between meals or a post training warmer. The soups in this section are really tasty, as well as being packed full of goodness. This is as easy and as nutritious as it gets.

All these soups require ordinary ingredients, which are easily available from any supermarket. Just about all England soup recipes have ten or less ingredients.

Other than a blender, no special equipment is required, although a microwave is very useful.

Time is valuable to us all, so to make the most of your time 'eat half and freeze half' is a good motto. If you cook twice the amount you need, then next time you will have homemade soup ready to de-frost and heat up in a minute. Many recipes show a short-cut where cooking time can be reduced by half. This means that a good number of soups take less than ten minutes to prepare and 7 minutes to cook. When pushed for time the 80/20 very quick soups show you how to pad out and enrich convenience soup with fresh vegetables.

Directions for making stocks are given to those who wish to use them. However, all these soups can be made with water and taste just as good.

Stocks

All the soups can be made with water and taste good. Nevertheless, for extra goodness they will benefit from a good chicken or vegetable stock. The recipes for both are given below.

Quick Vegetable Stock

Ingredients
1 stalk of celery with the leaves
2-3 carrots
1 onion or leek
Parsley stalks

Method
1. Coarsely chop the vegetables and brown in a large pan with a little oil.
2. Add 1¾pt (1 litre) of water and simmer gently for 30 minutes.
3. Strain. Either use now, or store in the fridge for 3-4 days or freeze.

Chicken Stock

Ingredients
Chicken carcass
Large onion, leek and carrot

Method
1. Break up the carcass of a roasted chicken. Put it in a large pan and cover with water, about 2-3 pints (1.2- 1.75 litres). Add a large onion or leek and perhaps a carrot if it is handy.
2. Simmer for 2-3 hours on a gentle heat. Do not allow to boil or the stock will go cloudy. Once cooked, strain the stock into another pan. Skim the fat off the surface.
3. Stock can be kept in the fridge for 3-4 days after which you need to boil it again for a few minutes, allow it to cool and then return it to the fridge. It can be kept indefinitely this way. Alternatively freeze it in batches.

Storage

Store Soups in a glass container in the fridge, avoid plastic and aluminium.

Freezing soups – eat half and freeze half
Making double the quantity of soup can reduce a lot of work. Every time you make soup eat half and freeze half. In practise you effectively cut down the overall work by 50%. This means that when you are pushed for time or just want a night off, you can have a home made nutritious soup that is ready in a few minutes.

Allow soups to cool properly before freezing. Use freezable containers and do not fill to the top because the liquid will expand by 10% when frozen. Alternatively use a robust freezer bag but make sure there is no moisture on the outside of the bag or it will stick to the inside of the freezer and tear when you try to get it out. Try freezing individual portions of soup in jam jars.

When defrosting, either leave the soup out to defrost at room temperature, or put into the microwave on 'defrost'. Do not sink any glassware into hot water or it will crack.

Quantities
All soup recipes serve four people which is about two good ladles each. Rugby players in training will need more.

Garnishes
Garnishes dress a soup, give it texture and make it visually interesting. Here are some choices:

Herbs – freshly chopped parsley, chives, coriander, thyme, marjoram, dill, fennel and basil can all be sprinkled over soups to make them interesting and enhance their flavour. If you have bought more than you require, store them in plastic bags in the freezer. Once thawed they will not have the same texture as fresh, but can be stirred into the soup straight from the freezer and brought to the boil without compromising the flavour. Alternatively, put large quantities of herbs in a food processor with some olive oil and process to a fine paste. Freeze as cubes in the ice tray.

Croutons – add crunch to soup. For simple croutons, pre-heat the oven to 200c/400F/Gas Mark 6. Slice the crusts off a loaf, preferably brown and then dice into half inch (1cm) cubes. Pour enough olive oil to just cover the bottom of a roasting dish and toss the bread cubes, so that they are coated in oil on all sides. Place in the oven, turning once every two minutes or so until they are golden. You can either keep them plain or sprinkle grated Parmesan all over them or even very finely chopped herbs like parsley. They can be frozen and reheated in the oven or grill when required.

Seeds – sunflower, pumpkin, and sesame can be ground in a blender and stored in a jamjar in the fridge, ready for use.

Nuts – flaked almonds, chopped cashew or ground pistachio can be added to or sprinkled over soups.

Adding Protein
To turn a simple soup into something more substantial-add some low fat protein. Ideas include 4oz (110g) of chopped chicken, egg, tuna, tofu pieces or left over red meat.

Broccoli and Courgette Soup with Parmesan

This soup tastes best with a mixture of broccoli and courgettes, but can be made exclusively with one or the other. The Parmesan along with the sharp taste of these green vegetables and nutmeg make natural partners. Make sure that you wash the broccoli well with a vegetable wash by adding few tablespoons of malt vinegar to the water or use "vegiwash" (available in good health food shops) Add some protein from the choices above to make a meal.

Serves 4
Time, 7 minutes preparation, 15 minutes cooking, 6 minutes shortcut
Freezes well

Ingredients

8 oz (225g) courgettes, chopped
8 oz (225g) broccoli, chopped
4 oz (110g) onion, chopped (1 medium onion)
1 clove of garlic, peeled and chopped
1tbs olive oil
1¼pt (750ml) stock or water
3oz (75g) grated Parmesan cheese
Good pinch of nutmeg
Salt and pepper to taste

Equipment – sharp knife and chopping board, blender, measuring jug, medium pan, (microwaveable dish and PVC free clingfilm)

Method

1. Chop the onion, garlic and vegetables finely. Grate the Parmesan.
2. Fry the chopped onion in a saucepan with the oil and garlic until the onion turns clear and is tender.
3. Add the nutmeg, stock/water, the chopped broccoli and courgettes. Bring to the boil then turn down to a simmer. Simmer for 10-15 minutes until the vegetables are tender but do not allow them to become a washed-out colour.
4. Remove from the heat and allow to cool a little. Add the grated Parmesan.
5. Liquidise in a blender until smooth and creamy.
6. Return to the pan and add a little more stock if necessary. Adjust the seasoning, garnish and serve.
7. Garnish with chopped seeds or a as a treat a swirl of crème fraiche with chopped chives.

Short-cut

To reduce the cooking time by half, put the chopped broccoli and courgettes into a microwaveable dish with a little water and cover with PVC free clingfilm. Cook on high for 5-6 minutes until they are tender. Remember the larger the slices, the longer they will take to cook.

Inside Knowledge
Broccoli is high in fibre, beta-carotene and folic acid. Courgettes provide some fibre.

Bacon and Lentil Soup

Bacon and lentil makes a sustaining winter soup. It is traditionally made from ham stock and dried lentils. This quick version uses bacon rashers instead of the ham stock and the tinned lentils reduce cooking time by hours.

Serves 4
Time, 7 minutes preparation 15 minutes cooking.
Shortcut, 6 minutes cooking.
Freezes well

Ingredients

4 rashers of lean smoked back bacon, chopped and rind removed
4oz (110g) finely chopped leek or onion. (one medium leek)
1tbs olive oil
2oz (50g) celery (about 2 sticks) finely sliced
2oz (50g) carrots finely sliced
400g tin of cooked, lentils
1¼ - 1½ pts (750- 900ml) stock or water
1 bay leaf (optional)

Equipment – tin opener, sharp knife and chopping board, blender, sieve, medium pan, measuring jug

Method

1. Take the rind and the fat off the bacon and chop it into small pieces. Fry it with the sliced leeks in a pan with the olive oil until the leeks are clear and tender.
2. Open the tin of lentils; rinse under the tap in a sieve and drain.
3. Add the lentils, the sliced carrots, celery, stock/water and bring to the boil. Turn down to a gentle simmer.
4. Simmer for about 15 minutes until the carrots and celery are tender. Remember the bigger the slices of celery the longer they will take to cook.
5. Allow to cool a little, remove the bay leaf and then put half the mixture into the blender. Liquidise until smooth. Put in the remainder for two or three seconds only. This will give a more interesting 'grainy' texture with a few whole lentils.
6. Return to the pan; add a little more stock if too thick. Adjust the seasoning, re-heat, garnish and serve.
7. Garnish with cheesy croutons and chopped parsley

Shortcut

To reduce cooking time put the carrots and celery in a microwaveable dish with a little water and cover with PVC free clingfilm. Cook on high for 6-7 minutes. This will reduce the cooking time by half.

Inside Knowledge
Lentils are a complex carbohydrate, high in fibre and contain some protein with a low GI. They contain some B vitamins and zinc. The bacon provides protein with relatively low fat as long as the fat and rind are removed.

Curried Lentil and Parsnip Soup With Coriander Raita

This is like a vegetable curry in a soup bowl. Serve it with coriander raita and either warm naan bread or poppadums for the full Indian effect.

Serves 4
Time, 12 minutes preparation, 15 minutes cooking
Freezes well

Ingredients

1tsp olive oil for frying
4oz (110g) chopped onion or leek (a medium leek or onion)
5oz (150g) tinned lentils
5oz (150g) parsnips, finely chopped
3oz (75g) apple, chopped (a medium apple)
2oz (50g) celery (about 2 sticks)
1 clove of garlic
1oz (25g) sultanas
1/4 pt (150ml) apple juice
1 1/4 pt (725ml) stock or water
1 tsp curry powder or paste

Garnish

5Tbs low fat plain bio-yoghurt,
5Tbs coriander, chopped
5Tbs semi-skimmed milk

Equipment, tin opener, sharp knife, chopping board, blender, spoon, medium pan, sieve, peeler, measuring jug

Method

1. Peel and chop the onions (or leeks) and the garlic. Peel and finely chop the parsnips and apple. Chop the celery.
2. Fry the leeks or onions in a pan with the oil and the curry powder until soft and clear. Do not burn.
3. Rinse and drain the lentils and weigh out 5 oz. Add the lentils, parsnips, celery, stock/water, apple and apple juice and sultanas to the pan. Bring to the boil and immediately turn down to a simmer for 15 minutes or until the parsnips are tender.
4. Remove from the heat, allow to cool a little and then liquidise leaving some of the mixture chunky.
5. Return to the heat. Add more stock if too thick, adjust the seasoning.
6. For the garnish mix the chopped coriander, yoghurt and milk into a cream and float on the soup. Serve.

Inside Knowledge
Lentils are complex carbohydrates and are high in fibre, B vitamins and zinc.They have a low GI and the parsnips have a high GI so this is a good soup to have after exercise. Yoghurt contains beneficial bacteria for gut health.

Mediterranean Bean and Tomato Soup

It is easy to transform the Tomato Soup with Basil recipe into this Mediterranean bean soup simply by adding a tin of haricot beans and varying the herbs a little. The beans add carbohydrate and some protein to make it a substantial meal. Increase the protein by adding some marinated tofu pieces. Instead of haricot, try butter beans.

Serves 4
Time, 5 minutes preparation, 10 minutes cooking
Freezes well

Ingredients

2tbs olive oil
8 oz (225g) onion, chopped
2 x 400g tins of chopped tomatoes
4tsp tomato puree
2 cloves of garlic, peeled and chopped
2oz (50g) carrots, sliced
1¼ pt (750ml) of water
1x 300g tin of haricot or other white beans.
Good pinch of fresh or dried thyme

Equipment, sharp knife, chopping board, tin opener, sieve, medium pan, measuring jug

Method

1. Peel and chop the onions and garlic and then fry them in a pan with the oil stirring now and then until clear and tender.
2. Stir in the tomato puree making sure it is well combined and then add the chopped tomatoes, herbs and water.
3. Put in the liquidiser and blend to a puree. Return to the pan.
4. Open the tin of beans, rinse with cold water and drain. Add to the soup along with the sliced carrots. Bring to the boil and then simmer for 10 minutes or until the carrots are tender.
5. Adjust the consistency and seasoning before serving with warm wholemeal pitta bread.

Inside Knowledge
Tomatoes provide beta-carotene, lycopene, and vitamins C and E. Both tinned tomatoes and puree contain more lycopene which is good for heart and prostate health. The beans are rich in protein. They contain dietary fibre which provide slow releasing energy.

Peanut and Pumpkin Soup

The bacon and peanuts complement each other and enhance the sweet taste of pumpkin. To fortify the soup, supplement 1/4 pt of water with semi-skimmed milk. If pumpkin is hard to come by, butternut squash will produce a similar result.

Serves 4
Time, 10 minutes preparation, 15 minutes cooking
Shortcut, 7 minutes
Freezes well

Ingredients

1tbs vegetable oil
4oz (110g) leek, chopped (1 medium leek)
4 lean back bacon rashers, rind removed
8oz (225g) pumpkin/ butternut squash cut into small cubes
3oz (75g) smooth peanut butter, preferably unsalted
1 1/4 - 1 1/2 pts (725-825ml) stock or water
1 clove garlic
pepper to taste

Equipment – sharp knife, chopping board, measuring jug, medium pan, blender, (microwaveable dish and PVC free clingfilm)

Method

1. Remove the rind and the fat from the bacon and chop. Wash and slice the leeks. De-seed and peel the pumpkin/squash and dice into 1/2" (1cm) cubes. Peel and chop the garlic.
2. Fry the chopped onion, garlic and bacon in a pan with the oil until the onion turns clear and is tender. Do not allow to brown.
3. Add the chopped pumpkin/squash, the peanut butter and the stock to the pan and simmer for 10-15 minutes or until the pumpkin/squash is tender.
4. Allow to cool a little. Liquidise half of the mixture until smooth and the other half for a few seconds only. This will give a more interesting consistency.
5. Return to the pan and reheat. Take care if you add salt as both the peanut butter and the bacon may be salted.

ShortCut

To reduce cooking time by half, put the small chunks of pumpkin/squash into a microwaveable dish with a little water and cover with PVC free clingfilm. Cook on high for 6-7 minutes until soft and tender. Transfer to a blender with the other ingredients.

Inside Knowledge
Pumpkin contains carotenoids. Peanuts are legumes and contain protein.

Tomato Soup with Basil

A simple and flavoursome tomato soup. It can be added to in a variety of ways to make many different soups. For instance, try adding sliced red pepper and an ounce or two of basmati rice. Any protein source will go well with this.

Serves 4
Time, 5 minutes preparation, 10 minutes cooking
Freezes well

Ingredients

2tbs olive oil
8oz (225g) chopped onion (1 good sized medium onion)
2 x 400g tins of chopped tomatoes
4tsp tomato puree
2 cloves of garlic, peeled and chopped
1tsp sugar
2tsp vinegar
1¼ pts (725ml) water
10 fresh basil leaves

Equipment, tin opener, sharp knife, chopping board, blender, medium pan, measuring jug

Method

1. Peel and chop the garlic and onion and then fry them in a pan, stirring now and then until the onion is clear and tender.
2. Stir in the tomato puree so that it is well combined with the onion and then add the tinned tomatoes, sugar, vinegar and stock/water.
3. Bring to the boil and then simmer for 10 minutes.
4. Allow to cool a little, before adding the fresh basil. Liquidise until smooth. Re-heat and serve.
5. Garnish with Parmesan shavings and a little extra basil or herbs, for a treat float a little crème fraiche.

Inside Knowledge
Tomatoes provide some beta-carotene, lycopene, potassium and vitamins C and E. Tinned tomatoes and puree contain more lycopene which is especially beneficial for prostate and heart health.

Minted Pea and Almond Soup

Sufficiently refined for the most formal of dinners, this soup is also very nourishing. It benefits from a good chicken stock, if you have time. Any protein will go with this dish.

Serves 4
Time, preparation 5 minutes, cooking 5 minutes
Freezes well

Ingredients

4oz (110g) onion, chopped (1 medium onion)
2oz (50g) leek, sliced (use the green part as well)
1tbs olive oil
2oz (50g) ground almonds
1pt (570ml) water or stock
8oz (225g) frozen, minted peas
salt and pepper to taste
a good handful of fresh mint

Equipment – sharp knife and chopping board, medium pan, measuring jug

Method

1. Chop the leeks and the onions finely and fry them with the oil in a pan, stirring now and then until they are clear and tender.
2. Add the ground almonds, the peas and the water/stock and simmer for 5 minutes or the cooking time specified on the pea packet.
3. Allow to cool a little and then put half the mixture in the blender and whizz until smooth and creamy- 10-15 seconds.
4. Put the remainder of the soup mixture with the fresh mint in the blender for about 5 seconds so that the mixture is rougher and the peas are 'grainy'.
5. Swill out the blender with a little water and add to the soup in the pan. Reheat, adjust the seasoning and serve.

Inside Knowledge
Peas are legumes which are a good carbohydrate source. They contain some vitamin C. Almonds are a source of protein and contain a range of minerals.

Carrot and Orange Soup with Fresh Ginger and Coriander

This soup bursts with colour and taste. The sesame seed oil gives it a distinctive oriental taste when combined with the ginger. For extra protein mild flavours are best; eggs, tofu, chicken or turkey breast.

Serves 4
Time, preparation 7 minutes, cooking 15 minutes, Shortcut 6 minutes
Freezes well

Ingredients

2tbs sesame seed oil or sunflower oil
4oz (110g) onion, chopped (one medium onion)
1 clove of garlic, peeled and chopped
1/2 inch (1cm) of fresh ginger, peeled and grated
1 1/2 - 2lb (700g-900g) fresh carrots, peeled and sliced
1pt (570ml) water/stock
1/4 pt (150ml) orange juice
handful of fresh coriander, roughly chopped
4tbs low-fat or bio yoghurt
4tbs milk

Equipment, sharp knife, chopping board, blender, peeler, medium pan, measuring jug

Method

1. Peel and chop the onion and garlic. Peel and grate the ginger. Fry them with the oil in a pan, stirring now and then until the onions turn clear. Do not burn or your soup will have brown bits in it.
2. Add the chopped carrots, the stock and the orange juice and simmer until the carrots are very tender, about 15 minutes.
3. Allow to cool a little. Transfer to the blender and liquidise until smooth.
4. Return to the pan and re-heat. Stir in the chopped coriander and serve immediately.
5. Garnish with the coriander and yoghurt by matching a tablespoon of yoghurt with a tablespoon of milk for every person and combine. Add chopped coriander to the mixture and float on the soup.

Shortcut

To reduce cooking time by 7 minutes, put the chopped carrots in a microwaveable dish, with a little water and cover with PVC free clingfilm. Cook on high for 6-7 minutes until the carrots are tender. Add to the stock and orange juice and put through the blender.

Inside Knowledge
Carrots are rich in beta-carotene which converts in the body to Vitamin A. Ginger aids digestion and the coriander contains coumarins.

Celery and Pistachio Soup

The two greens give this soup a beautiful colour and it is creamy and crunchy at the same time. Ham as an additional protein will complement the celery.

Serves 4
Time, 7 minutes preparation, 15 minutes cooking
Shortcut, 7 minutes cooking
Freezes well

Ingredients

1tbs sunflower or olive oil
4oz (110g) onion, finely chopped, (1 medium)
8oz (225g) celery finely sliced (about 3 sticks)
2oz (50g) pistachio nuts, natural, unsalted, shelled
1¼ pt (725ml) stock or water
1tsp fennel

Equipment - sharp knife, chopping board, medium pan, measuring jug, blender

Method

1. Put the shelled, unsalted pistachio nuts in a blender and whizz until powder. Peel and chop the onion and slice the celery into thin slices. (Celery can take some time to cook, reduce this by cutting it in thin slices)
2. Fry the chopped onion with the oil in a pan, stirring now and then until the onion is clear and tender. Do not brown.
3. Add the celery, the ground pistachios, the stock/water and fennel and simmer gently for 15 minutes.
4. Allow to cool slightly then blend until smooth or leave some of the mixture chunky.
5. Return to the pan. Adjust the taste and consistency, reheat and serve.

Shortcut

To reduce cooking time by half, put the sliced celery into a microwaveable dish with a little water and cover with PVC-free clingfilm. Cook on high for 6-7 minutes or until the celery is tender. Return to the pan and blend as above.

Inside Knowledge
Celery is a mild diuretic and is rich in phytochemicals. Pistachio nuts provide some protein and minerals.

80/20 Very Quick Fresh Soups

Following the 80/20 rule remember that even If you are pushed for time, you can still get the benefits of fresh vegetables by padding out a convenience soup. Choose soups that are low in fat. Avoid 'cream of' varieties, and choose those naturally high in vegetables and pulses. Fresh soups in cartons are preferable, although be aware that they come in different sizes, so a little judgement with the quantities is required. If fresh soup is not available use tinned or packet.

Very Quick Leek and Potato Soup

Servings – see the number on the carton or tin
Time, 5 minutes preparation, 2 minutes cooking

Can be frozen, but check the carton and date

Ingredients

1tbs sunflower or olive oil
1 carton of fresh leek and potato soup
1 medium leek, finely sliced
1/4 pt (150ml) of semi-skimmed milk
good pinch of nutmeg
1tbs fresh chives

Equipment - sharp knife, chopping board, scissors, medium pan

Method

1. Snip the chives with scissors. Wash and slice the leek very finely. Fry the leek in a pan with the oil until tender and clear.
2. Add the convenience soup to the pan along with the chives and nutmeg.
3. Stirring all the time add the milk to the consistency you like. If you prefer a smooth soup allow it to cool a little and then put it through the blender. Reheat and serve.

Inside Knowledge
Leeks are mildly diuretic. They belong to the same family as garlic and onions and so may help reduce blood cholesterol. Potatoes are a good source of carbohydrate and potassium.

80/20, Very Quick Mushroom Soup

Most supermarkets produce interesting packs of different mushrooms including; Girolles, Oyster, Paris Brown, Button, Horse and Portabello all of which can add interest in taste and texture as well as fresh nutrition. Add some protein to this for a nourishing soup.

Servings – see the number on the carton
Time, 5 minutes preparation,
2 minutes cooking.
Can be frozen but check the carton and date

Ingredients

1 carton of fresh convenience mushroom soup
5oz (150g) of fresh mushrooms
1/4 pt (150ml) semi-skimmed milk
2 spring onions
1tbs olive oil
1tbs fresh parsley

Equipment, sharp knife, chopping board, medium pan

Method

1. Wash and chop the mushrooms. Finely slice the spring onions. Chop the parsley.
2. Fry the mushrooms and the spring onions on a medium heat for a few minutes until the mushrooms have lost some of their water.
3. Add the convenience soup. Stirring all the time add the milk to the consistency you desire.
4. Add the parsley and serve. It you want a fine soup, allow to cool a little then put through the blender.

Inside Knowledge
Mushrooms contain potassium. Shiitake mushrooms contain phytochemicals which are good for immunity. Parsley contains traces of calcium, iron, potassium and vitamins A and C.

Shopping Check-list for Soups

Refer to this list every time you go shopping to make sure you have the necessary ingredients to make your soups.

Fresh Vegetables
Courgettes
Broccoli
Onions
Garlic
Leeks
Carrots
Parsnips
Pumpkin
Red peppers
Spring onions
Mushrooms, various
Celery
Butternut squash

Frozen Vegetables
Minted frozen peas

Fresh Herbs and Spices
Mint
Coriander
Parsley
Chives
Basil
Fennel or Dill
Thyme
Marjoram
Bay
Ginger

Fresh Fruits
Lemons
Limes
Apple

Tins and Tubes
400g organic lentils
400g chopped tomatoes
400g haricot, butter, white beans, lentils or others you prefer.
Tomato paste - tube
Coconut milk - small

Oils
(buy in glass bottles and store in the fridge)
Olive oil, extra virgin first cold pressing
Sesame seed, small
Sunflower oil (first pressing)

Dairy
Parmesan/Pecorino cheese
Low fat, plain or bio yoghurt
Semi-skimmed milk
Eggs

Grains
Basmati rice

Spices
Nutmeg
Curry powder

Nuts and Seeds
Ground almonds
Pistachio, shelled and unsalted
Pumpkin seeds
Sunflower seeds

Meat
Lean Back Bacon
Chicken bones for stock
Chicken or turkey breast, ham, lamb, beef or game

Juices
Orange juice
Apple juice

Miscellaneous
Ready made hummus
Peanut butter, organic, smooth,
Bread for croutons
Vinegar
Sugar

it's cool to cook - introducing the team

Martin Johnson

The Rugger Burgger

The combination of beef and nuts provides a good source of protein. Make it with the best organic lean beef and try to use fresh parsley because the taste is so much better. Serve it on a toasted wholemeal bap. Garnish with a slice of low fat cheese or any of the traditional burger accompaniments such as dill pickle, fresh onion rings, a slice of tomato or lettuce. Make large amounts and freeze them, so that all you have to do is take out and de-frost. If you enjoy burgers regularly then every time you finish a loaf, just whizz up the crust to make breadcrumbs. Store them in a plastic bag in the freezer and use them when you need to.

Serves 4 (four quarter pound burgers)
Time, 12 minutes preparation, 7 minutes cooking
Freezes well,

Ingredients

1lb (450g) freshly minced lean organic beef
1 large fresh egg
4oz (110g) onion, chopped (1 medium onion)
4tbs tomato ketchup
3tbs fresh parsley, chopped
1oz (25g) pistachio nuts, shelled, non-salted
1oz (25g) brown breadcrumbs
1tsp English mustard
Worcestershire sauce, a good dash
salt to taste, about ½ tsp max.

Equipment – blender, sharp knife, chopping board, mixing bowl, frying pan

Method

1. Put the pistachio nuts in the blender and whizz until mainly powder.
2. Chop up 1oz (25g) of brown bread into cubes and whizz until it crumbs.
3. Chop the onion and the parsley.
4. Put the egg, the onion, the parsley, ketchup, mustard, Worcestershire and salt in the blender and whizz until puree.
5. Put the beef and the breadcrumbs into the mixing bowl and then add the mixture from the blender and combine together. Best done with clean hands.
6. Shape into four burgers and fry them with a little oil until light brown on both sides and cooked in the middle.

Phil Vickery

Inside Knowledge
A good source of protein with iron, zinc and B vitamins. Just over half of lean beef's calories are from fat, although only half is saturated. Onions contain some quercitin, an antioxidant.

All Souped-Up - Hummus and Butternut Squash Soup

This soup is quick to make and is wonderfully nutritious. Make it in large quantities and freeze it in batches to be taken out at a moment's notice. It can be made with pumpkin if squash is not available.

Serves 4
Time, 6 minutes preparation, 15 minutes cooking
Short cut, 7 minutes

Ingredients

4 oz (110g) onion, chopped, (a medium onion)
1 lb (450g) butternut squash, seeded and chopped
1¼ pt (725ml) of water or stock
6oz (175g) tub of hummus
1tbs olive oil
1 garlic clove
cinnamon, pinch
1tbs parsley, flat leafed

Equipment – sharp knife, chopping board, microwaveable dish, non pvc clingfilm, blender, wooden spoon, medium pan

Method

1. Chop the onion and garlic and fry in a pan with the oil until tender and clear. Do not allow to burn.
2. Peel and de-seed the squash and cut it into ½" (1 cm) small chunks. Add to the pan with the stock and the hummus and simmer for 15 minutes until the squash is tender.
3. Remove from the heat and allow to cool a little. Put into the blender in batches and whizz until smooth and creamy.
4. Add salt and pepper to taste, a good pinch of cinnamon and garnish with flat leafed parsley or herby croutons.

Short Cut

To reduce cooking time by half, put the chunks of squash into a microwaveable dish with a little water in the bottom and cover with clingfilm. Cook on high for 6-7 minutes until the squash is tender. Transfer to the blender along with the other ingredients.

Inside Knowledge
Pumpkin contains the carotenoid phytoene. The hummus which is made of chickpeas and tahini provides the nutrients that make up protein and contains some calcium, and traces of other minerals. The chick peas have a low GI. This soup is extremely nutritious.

Try Thai

Coconut milk is good news. Although a saturated fat it is of a type used for energy and not stored as fat. You do need a good chicken stock for this. The average rugby player may eat two chicken breasts alone so you will need to increase quantities accordingly.

Serves 4
Time, 15 minutes preparation, 10 minutes cooking

Ingredients

2 -3 chicken breasts
1 x tin 425g of coconut milk
3/4 pt (425ml) good chicken stock
4 spring onions, finely chopped
4 stalks lemon grass or grated rind of 1/2 lemon
4 small red chillies
juice of 1 lime
1tsp fresh ginger, grated
2tsp soy sauce
2tbs fresh coriander, chopped

Equipment – sharp knife, chopping board, grater, medium pan

Method

1. Slice the chicken breasts into thin strips.
2. If using lemon grass, cut the base of each stalk, peel the outer layers and chop only the bottom 4" of each stalk. Throw the rest away. If using lemon rind instead, grate the zest.
3. Slice the spring onions finely. Slice the red chillies lengthways, and remove the seeds. Grate the ginger and juice the limes. Chop the coriander and keep it to the end.
4. Put the stock, the coconut milk, the spring onions, lemon rind, chillies, soy sauce and ginger into a pan. Bring to simmering point and add the chicken. Simmer gently for 10 minutes until cooked. Do not boil
5. Add the coriander and serve immediately

Inside Knowledge
Chicken is a good source of low fat protein. Coconut milk contains calcium and magnesium as well as traces of many other minerals. It contains medium chain triglycerides which are a useful energy source for athletes. The limes are rich in bioflavonoids.

Pick Your Own Pocket

Here are four fillings for wholemeal pitta pockets. Alternatively, make the combinations into a main meal salad. Servings are for one so they are easy to multiply.

Wholemeal Pitta pockets make an excellent sandwich because you can pack lots of filling into them and eat them on the go. If pushed for time, make larger amounts of filling and keep it in in a covered bowl in the fridge for 2-3 days. Make up pockets as you need them. Each pocket filling delivers a 'complete meal' in terms of carbohydrate and protein. So even if you have little time, you will be nourishing yourself.

Line Your Pocket With Leaves

Toast the pockets for about 1½ minutes in the toaster so that it is a light brown on both sides but not burned or hard. With a sharp knife and your hands on the top of the pocket to steady it, slit it from 'ear to ear' so that top half of the seam stays untouched and the bottom half is open. Gently force the bread apart without tearing, to make a pocket.

Pitta Pocket - Smoked Salmon With Fresh Chives, Egg and Lemon Mayo

Serves one pocket
Time, 5 minutes

Ingredients

2-3oz (60g-75g) strip of smoked salmon
1 boiled egg, peeled and chopped (add extra egg white for more protein)
1tbs very low fat mayonnaise
1tbs low fat plain or bio yoghurt
1tbs fresh chives, chopped
squeeze of lemon

Equipment – sharp knife, chopping board, scissors and mixing bowl

Method

1. Mix the mayonnaise and yoghurt together and then squeeze in some lemon.
2. With a pair of scissors snip the chives and the smoked salmon into a bowl.
3. Chop up the boiled egg.
4. Mix all the ingredients together and stuff your pocket !

Inside Knowledge

Salmon is high in Omega 3 oils which are cardio protective and important for brain function and memory. It is an excellent source of protein. Egg is also a protein. The yoghurt contains beneficial bacteria, for bowel health. The chives contain vitamin C, and some beta-carotene. Wholemeal pitta is a source of B vitamins.

Pitta Pocket - Spicy Chicken With Almonds and Apricots

Use any left-over chicken for this. Don't miss out the apricots as they go well with the spices and nuts as well as being a good source of iron.

Serves One
Time, 5 minutes

Ingredients

3-4oz (75g-110g) cooked chicken (add more to increase protein intake)
1 ready to eat dried apricot
1 spring onion
1tbs flaked almonds or pine nuts
1tbs very low fat mayonnaise
1tbs low fat plain bio yoghurt
1/2 tsp curry paste or powder

Equipment – sharp knife, mixing bowl, chopping board, teaspoon

Method

1. Mix the mayonnaise, yoghurt and curry paste in a bowl until they are well combined.
2. Chop up the chicken, spring onion, and apricot.
3. Put them in the bowl along with the almonds and mix.
4. Fill the pocket.

Jonny Wilkinson and brother Mark

Inside Knowledge
Chicken is a good low fat protein which is required for muscle growth and repair. Yoghurt contains beneficial bacteria for the maintenance of the intestinal tract. The lemon contains some vitamin C. Apricots are a good source of iron.

Pitta Pocket - Smoked Mackerel With Horseradish Mayonnaise and Grapes

The peppery taste of the horseradish enhances the oiliness of the mackerel. Line your pocket with rocket leaves for this one.

Use tinned tuna instead of the mackerel for a change and add some chopped red onion if you like it.

Serves one
Time, 5 minutes

Ingredients

3-4oz (75g-110g) plain smoked mackerel
5 seedless grapes
½ tbs horseradish sauce
1½ tbs plain, low fat yoghurt
1 spring onion

Equipment – spoon, bowl, sharp knife, chopping board

Inside Knowledge
Mackerel contains omega 3 oils which are anti-inflammatory and good for cardiac health. It is a source of protein and therefore required for muscle growth and repair. Horseradish contains protective phytochemicals and some vitamin C. Onion contains the flavonoid, quercetin. Red grapes contain polyphenols, the same as those in red wine. They also contain ellagic acid, a useful phytochemical.

Method

1. Mix the horseradish sauce and the yoghurt into a bowl.
2. Flake the mackerel from its skin into the bowl with your thumb, taking care to spot the odd bone.
3. Quarter the grapes and chop up the spring onion.
4. Combine all the ingredients and fill the pocket.

Danny Grewcock

Pitta Pocket - Raw Beetroot With Feta and Walnuts

This dish should be seen as a bit of a treat, as it is relatively low in protein and fairly high in fat.

Most people have not eaten beetroot raw, but once they do they wonder why we have eaten it cooked with vinegar for all these years. Raw beetroot is full of health and flavour – its sweet taste responds to a squeeze of lemon. Use Roquefort if you do not have Fetta or any goat's cheese that is sharp and chalky.

Serves one
Time, 5 minutes

Ingredients

2oz (50g) raw beetroot, grated
2oz (50g) Fetta cheese
1tbs broken walnut pieces
1tbs chives
squeeze of lemon

Equipment – scissors, mixing bowl, grater, spoon

Inside Knowledge
Beetroot is a good source of folic acid. The fibre from the wholemeal pocket provides some fibre. Beetroot also contains some beta-carotene. The cheese is a source of protein but high in fat so go easy. Walnuts are rich in polyunsaturates, zinc and may help as part of a cholesterol reducing diet.

Method

1. Peel and grate the fresh beetroot. Break up the feta cheese and the walnuts. Snip the chives with the scissors.
2. Combine in a mixing bowl with a squeeze of lemon and then fill the pocket.

Crudités – Dip Into Our Exposé of Raw Talent

Crudités are raw vegetables eaten with a dip, usually as a starter or with an aperitif.

Crudités

Cut into chunks any number of the following vegetables. Arrange them on a plate with the dip in the middle. Accompany with warm pitta bread, naan (although these are high in fat!) or papadams.
Eat as many colours as you can! Red, yellow, green or orange peppers, carrots, celery, fennel, cucumber, cauliflower, broccoli, radishes, courgettes, spring onions, cherry tomatoes, red onions, olives.

Nutrition power - Each colour has its own power!

Colour	Content	Benefit
green	chlorophyll and magnesium	nerves, muscle, hormones
yellow	cartenoids	cancer protecting
orange	beta-carotene, lycopene	anti-ageing, male health
red	anti-oxidants	heart
red/dark	flavenoids, antioxidants	anti-ageing

Aubergine Dip

Pick a good, firm aubergine with dark, glossy skin. Purists will want to roast it whole in the oven. It will take 30 minutes at 200c /400f /Gas Mark 6 and you will need two aubergine because they lose all their moisture. The quick route, however, is set out below.

Serving, One dip with 8oz (225g) raw vegetables serves four people.
Time, 12 minutes preparation, 6 minutes cooking

Ingredients

1 aubergine
2 lemons
1tbs olive oil
1-2 cloves of garlic
good pinch paprika
2tbs parsley, chopped

Equipment – peeler, sharp knife, chopping board, blender, microwaveable dish, clingfilm, spoon, spatula, garlic press, serving bowl

Method

1. Peel the aubergine with a peeler and chop it into small cubes. Put it in a microwaveable dish and squeeze the juice of a lemon over it making sure that it coats all the cubes (best done with clean hands). This stops the aubergine from discolouring. Cover with pvc-free clingfilm and microwave on high for 3 minutes, stir the contents and repeat. When ready, the aubergine should have collapsed, losing all its springiness and become transparent. If not put it in the microwave again.

2. Peel a clove of garlic, or two and put it through the garlic press. Put the garlic, the olive oil and the lemon juice in the blender and whizz until it becomes a milky liquid.

3. Now add half of the cooked aubergine to the blender and whizz until it becomes a puree. Transfer to a serving bowl. Puree the remainder in the blender and transfer that to the serving bowl too. Mix well, cover the bowl and put it in the fridge to cool. Before serving add the chopped flat leafed parsley.

Inside Knowledge

Aubergines have a range of vitamins and minerals but only in small quantities. Most people salt away the bitter juices but it is they that contain the nutrients. Cooked garlic does not have the same properties as fresh but is still very effective and contains an antioxidant that can help prevent heart disease. The lemon juice contains some vitamin C.

Hummus and Pepper Dip

Use the colourful peppers like the orange, red or yellow for this dip. The green would make it dull in colour. By padding out the hummus with the pepper, the fat content per finished spoonful is reduced by half.

One dip with vegetables serves four as a starter
Time, 7 minutes preparation, 4 minutes cooking

Ingredients

1/2 pepper (red, orange or yellow)
6oz (175g) tub of hummus

Equipment – sharp knife, chopping board, serving bowl, blender, microwaveable dish

Method

1. Cut the pepper in half and de-seed it. Chop it into small cubes.
2. Put it in a microwaveable dish with a tablespoon of water and cover with clingfilm. Cook on high for 3-4 minutes until tender.
3. Transfer to the blender and whizz to a puree.
4. Add to the hummus. Cover and transfer to the fridge to cool before serving.

Neil and Olivia Back

Inside Knowledge
The hummus contains chickpeas and tahini which together provide an alternative protein source to meat. The sweet pepper contains some beta carotene, and small amounts of other antioxidant vitamins.

Avocado Dip

Avocados should be soft, buttery and golden inside. They are nutritionally rich especially in vitamin E and monosaturated fats.

One dip with vegetables serves four as a starter
Time, 10 minutes

Ingredients

6oz (175g) avocado (about 2 medium)
2oz (50g) green pepper
juice of 1 lemon
1tbs olive oil
salt and pepper
1-2 garlic cloves
paprika

Equipment – sharp knife, chopping board, garlic press, blender, serving bowl

Inside Knowledge
Avocados. They are rich in Omega 6 polyunsaturated fat and vitamin E. The olive oil contains omega 9 oil, a monounsaturated fat. The garlic aids digestion and has been shown to help protect against heart disease.

Method

1. Peel the avocado and take out the stone. Chop it into small chunks.
2. De-seed the pepper and chop up 2 oz (50g) into very small cubes.
3. Peel the garlic and put it through the garlic press or chop it up very finely.
4. Put the lemon juice, the olive oil, and the garlic into the blender and give it a whizz until it becomes a milky liquid.
5. Add the green pepper and blend to a puree. Then add the avocado, half at a time.
6. Put the resulting pale green puree into a serving dish. Cover with clingfilm and cool in the fridge until required. Give a sprinkling of paprika before serving.

Matt Perry

The Destroyer – Helps to Flatten a Cold or Hangover

Ginger and mint are very good for settling upset stomachs. The orange and lemon juice delivers fresh vitamin C which can help to support the immune system and is good for both hangovers and a cold. This is also great when warmed up a little.

Serves One

Ingredients

1 oz (25g) fresh, finely chopped or grated ginger
10fl oz (150mls) fresh orange juice, (freshly squeezed)
juice of 1 lemon
large sprig of mint

Kieran and Victoria Bracken

Method

1. Peel and grate the ginger, squeeze the oranges and lemons.

1. Put the ginger, mint and a couple of fluid ounces of the orange juice in the blender and liquidise so that all ingredients are well combined. Add the rest of the orange juice.

2. This will keep in the refrigerator but the vitamin C will decline rapidly so it is best to make and consume it immediately. Ginger like garlic becomes more fiery over time. For added immune support add soluable vitamin C.

Inside Knowledge

Ginger is a good aid to digestion and settles a stomach and stops you feeling sick as does the mint. Ginger is fiery, stimulating and anti-bacterial. The orange juice, if fresh, will replace the lost vitamin C if you have been out on the razzle, or give support to the immune system if you have a cold. Either way you will probably want to take an aspirin.

The Austin Healey Big Mouth Bacon Butty

You have to have a really large mouth to eat this. The ordinary man can probably manage three slices, but Austin, who is particularly gifted, can fit four.

Serves one
Time, 10 minutes

Ingredients

4 slices of wholemeal bread, toasted
1-2 tomatoes, sliced
9 slices of lean bacon with the fat removed
1tbs reduced fat mayonnaise
1tbs low fat, plain bio yoghurt
As much brown sauce as you like but remember it is high in sugar

Equipment – sharp knife and chopping board, spoon, small mixing bowl

Method

1. Slice up the tomato and put it under the grill along with the 9 slices of lean bacon with the fat removed.
2. Put the four slices of bread in the toaster.
3. Mix the mayonnaise and the yoghurt together.
4. Lay three slices of bread down on the work surface. Spread them with the yoghurt mixture first, then the sliced tomatoes and thirdly the bacon in three equal quantities. Finish with a good whack of brown sauce over each slice. Stack the slices ending with the fourth on top. Open your mouth as wide as you can.

Austin and Louise Healey

Inside Knowledge
This butty is relatively low in fat if the rind and fat are cut off the bacon. The tomatoes contain lycopene which is a good antioxidant. The brown bread contains some fibre and B vitamins.

Phil Greening

What is Hot, Fast and Green?
Answer - This vegetable curry.

This curry sauce freezes well. Make double the amount. Eat half and freeze half . Store in a screw –top jar in the freezer. Just make sure they are labelled and do not get them mixed up with the tomato sauce for pasta (!) Remember to freeze jars with the lid off until frozen because liquid expands at 10%. Do not re-heat quickly or the glass will crack.

Add 3-4 chicken breasts instead of the vegetables to make this into a protein meal.

Serves 4
Time 10 minutes preparation, 20 minutes cooking
Freezes well

Ingredients

4oz (110g) onion, (one medium onion)
2tbs sunflower oil
1x 400g tin chopped tomatoes
1 clove garlic
1 apple, diced
2tbs mild curry paste
1oz (25g) ground almonds
8-10tbs coconut milk
4oz (110g) peas or mangetout
4oz (110g) broccoli
4oz (110g) courgettes
8oz (225g) basmati or brown rice

Equipment – sharp knife and chopping board, 2 medium pans

Method

1. Peel and finely chop the onion, the garlic and the apple. Fry in a pan with 2tbs of sunflower seed oil until the onion turns clear and tender.
2. Add the curry paste and stir in well. Add the tin of tomatoes and the coconut milk. Simmer with the lid on (because is splatters) for ten minutes.
3. Meanwhile chop the courgettes, weigh out the frozen peas or mangetout and break up the broccoli. Put the salted water on for the rice.
4. Add the vegetables and simmer for another ten minutes. Add the rice to the boiling water. Cook for the time on the packet, drain and serve with the curry.

Inside Knowledge
The tomatoes contain lycopene which is a very good antioxidant. The almonds contain some calcium, magnesium and zinc as does the coconut milk.

Tackle This! - Warm Salad of Poached Egg on Smoked Haddock

The joy of this dish is the warm golden egg yolk gently spreading over the fish. If you are going to poach your eggs the proper way, you need eggs that are very fresh. Alternatively you can use an egg poacher, but it usually makes the egg whites rubbery so they slide off the fish. To increase low fat protein add extra egg whites.

Serves 4
Time, preparation 7 minutes, cooking time 12 minutes

Ingredients

4 x 4oz (125g) smoked haddock fillets
4 eggs, fresh, large
4tbs olive oil
2tbs balsamic vinegar
8oz (225g) baby spinach and/or rocket
1tbs fresh chives
1tbs ordinary vinegar

Equipment – frying pan, medium pan, small pan, sharp knife and chopping board

Method

1. Arrange the salad leaves on four plates and set aside. Chop the chives.
2. Put a frying pan on the heat with about 2" of water in it and add a dash of ordinary vinegar. Bring it to the boil and then turn the heat right down so that the water is bubbling very, very gently. Break each egg individually into a cup and slide one by one into the water. Simmer the eggs for just one minute. Take the pan off the heat and leave them to continue cooking whilst you are poaching the fish. The eggs will be perfectly cooked in eight minutes, but do not leave them any longer.
3. When you take the eggs off the heat place the haddock into a saucepan and cover with water. Bring to the boil, and immediately turn the heat down and simmer for 4-5 minutes until the fish is cooked.
4. Whilst the fish is cooking and the eggs are resting, put the olive oil, the chives and vinegar in a small pan and heat till it bubbles.
5. Everything should be about ready so you need to work quickly. With a slotted spoon, place the haddock in the centre of each plate. (Make sure you allow everything to drain properly). Remove the poached eggs and place them on top of the haddock. Spoon the dressing over. Serve immediately.

Inside Knowledge
Fish and eggs provide a good source of protein, although the yolks contain all the fat. Spinach is a good source of fibre but not rich in iron as some believe. It contains oxalic acid which can hinder the absorption of calcium and iron but is a good source of beta carotene and the carotenoid lutein, good for eye health.

A Little Bit of What You Fancy............ Apple Crumble

This is high fat, high carbohydrate. Serve it with lashings of cream and enjoy it - it's the only high fat recipe in the book. But we follow the 80/20 rule which allows treats. Add 2oz (50g) of ground almonds to the mixture if you like them, they give it a different texture and taste.

The crumble mixture freezes well so you can make it in advance if you want to.

Serves 4
Time- preparation 10 minutes, cooking 20-25 mins.
Freezes well

Ingredients

8oz (225g) plain flour
4oz (110g) caster sugar
4oz (110g) white or brown breadcrumbs
6oz (175g) butter
2lbs (900g) cooking apples
good dash of cinnamon

Equipment – peeler, sharp knife and chopping board, mixing bowl or (food processor), shallow oven dish

Method

1. Put the oven on to 180c/350f/Gas Mark 4
2. Put the butter, flour, sugar, almonds and breadcrumbs either in the food processor and process to a light crumbly mixture, or combine by hand in a mixing bowl.
3. Peel and core the apples. Slice them and put them immediately in a microwaveable dish with a little water on the bottom. Shake a little cinnamon over them . Cover with clingfilm and cook on high for about 5 minutes. Take out, stir and put them back in for another 3 minutes if still hard.
4. Spread the apple mixture on the bottom of a shallow oven dish. Sprinkle the crumble mixture over them . Do this just before you put them into the oven, or the crumble will get soggy. Bake for 20 - 25 minutes.
5. Serve with extra thick double cream... and enjoy.

Inside Knowledge
The apples contain pectin which is good for eliminating toxins. They have a low GI.

Pennyhill Park

The Pennyhill Park Hotel and Country Club is the home of England Rugby training. Over the last two years, head chef Karl Edmunds and soux chef Dave Campbell have worked exceptionally hard to ensure that the food at Pennyhill meets the exacting standards of Roz Kadir from CNM, Dave Reddin from England Rugby, and most importantly, the players.

Food during a test match week must satisfy a number of important requirements.

1. It must be nutritionally excellent and provide the energy and nutrients players need to cope with and recover from the demands of heavy training.
2. It must be simple and recognisable! Players like to eat familiar things during test week preparation – not too many suprises.
3. It must taste fantastic and have enough variety to satisfy all of the different tastes in the squad.

Karl and Dave at Pennyhill have done a fantastic job in ensuring this is the case. Maybe this is one of the secrets of a great winning run since the team have stayed at Pennyhill.

We are always being asked what the players really eat during a test week. Following is a typical menu for a day at Pennyhill Park when England are staying.

Breakfast
Fruit Juices
Still Mineral water
Selection of fresh fruit – melon, strawberries, raspberries, grapes
Selection of organic cereals – low sugar
Organic porridge oats
Lean back bacon steaks
Sugar free baked beans
Grilled tomatoes
Grilled mushrooms
Poached eggs
Egg white omelettes – 3 whites to 1 yolk – with various fillings
Wholemeal toast

Lunch
Lentil and ham hock soup with winter vegetables
Lightly peppered smoked salmon
Caesar salad
Sliced beef tomato with fennel and roasted pepper salad

Shepherds pie with honey roasted root vegetables
Risotto of chicken with Italian tomatoes, Black pepper and Mediterranean veg.
Savoy cabbage with bacon
Large mixed salad

Apricot and sultana filo money parcels
Large basket of fresh fruit

Afternoon Snacks
Large wholemeal sandwiches to include low fat beef, turkey, ham, tuna, with salad
Large basket of fruit
Protein bars

Dinner
Hot and sour soup with glass noodles
Chicken and tiger prawns
Grilled flat mushrooms with tomato salsa
Avocado and smoked bacon salad
Lamb curry with cauliflower, spinach and Bombay alloo
Brown Basmati rice
Grilled salmon steaks with minted new potatoes & panache of seasonal veg.
Large mixed salad

Low fat steamed chocolate pudding with low fat crème fraiche
Large basket of fruit

Evening Snacks
Lightly salted popcorn
Ryvita and rice cakes
Hummus, guacamole & salsa
Selection of mixed nuts and raisins
Smoked chicken Caesar Salad

raw talent

The Great Green Salad

A good green salad is the cornerstone of a healthy diet. Create your own salad from the list of ingredients below. Use it as a shopping check-list and a creative prompt. Keep a running stock of green vegetables changing them all the time so that you have a choice of endless combinations. Make a different salad dressing each week. Eat vegetables that are in season.

Rough Guide To Creating Green Salads

Formula (serves one)
Take the following formula as a very rough guide for creating a balanced green salad;

2oz leaves + 2oz veg + 2tbs herbs + 2tbs seeds + 2tbs dressing

Take at least one ingredient from each column and begin to create your own green salad. This list is not exhaustive but it will enable you to see the many combinations.

Ingredients

Leaves +	Herbs +	Vegetables +	Oils +	Vinegars +	Seeds/Nuts
Kos	Chives	Asparagus	Olive	White wine	Pumpkin
Iceberg	Parsley	Avocado	Hazelnut	Red Wine	Sunflower
Endive	Basil	Gr Pepper	Pumpkin	Cider	Sesame
Spinach	Coriander	Sp Onion	Walnut	Balsamic	Pistachio
Lambs L.	Fennel	Gr Olives	Sunflower	Sherry	Cumin
Watercress	Sorrel	Celery	Rapeseed	Raspberry	Pecan
Rocket	Mint	Courgette	Peanut	Basil	Hazlenut
Dandelion	Rosemary	French Bean	Linseed	Lavender	Cashew
Cress	Sage	Broad Bean	Flax Seed	Rosemary	Pine

Method
The formula above serves one. Multiply it by the number of people you are serving if you want more.

1. Tear the leaves up with your hands to bite-sized bits or whatever size you want. Put the leaves on the plate.
2. Select a herb and chop it up, either roughly or finely. Scatter it over the leaves.
3. You will need about 2oz(50g) per person of green vegetables, so if you select two vegetables then they you will need about 1oz (25g) of each. Chop finely or roughly or keep whole.
4. Make the dressing. A basic vinaigrette is 3 parts oil to 1 part vinegar. Add salt to taste.
5. Add about 2tbs of dressing to the salad and toss the ingredients. Finish with a sprinkling of seeds or nuts.

Endless Combinations

From the list above you can get over 2,000 different combinations of green salad! Here are three to start you off....

- Baby spinach, mint with asparagus. Hazelnut with lemon dressing and cashew nut sprinkle
- Lambs lettuce, chives and avocado with sunflower and cider dressing and a scattering of sesame seeds.
- Dandelion (found in most gardens!), dill and broad bean with walnut and sherry dressing and a sprinkling of pistachio nuts.

Over to you !

Keeping Your Leaves For Longer

We all have that bag of 'designer leaves' quietly wilting in the bottom of our fridge. When you buy made-up salad leaves from the supermarket, just take them out of the packet when you get home and refresh them with a little water. Re-seal the pack with a clothes peg or fastener and store it in the bottom of the fridge. You will find that refreshing will extend their life for a few days more. Do not allow water to collect in the bottom of the bag or the leaves will rot.

Herbs

Some herbs are stronger than others. Sage, rosemary and thyme are quite pungent and should therefore be used with a little caution, whilst mint, parsley, chives and basil are milder and can be used with less restraint. Each herb has its own beneficial nutritional properties so do try a wide variety. Use fresh herbs whenever possible.

Cooked Green Vegetables

Some green vegetables benefit from being cooked. Asparagus, broad beans and French beans in particular. Put what you require in a microwaveable dish with a little water in the bottom. Cover with clingfilm and cook on high for 3 minutes. Alternatively steam them. Whichever way, take out and refresh with lots of cold water to stop the cooking process. Pat dry and use.

Seeds and Nuts

Put one or a combination of seeds and nuts in a blender and whizz until grainy. Keep in a screw-top jar in the fridge and sprinkle on to salads and soups when you wish. They are delicious whole, so nibble a few with a power drink.

Compound Salads – Turn a Simple Salad into a Meal

To turn a simple green salad into a full meal all you have to do is add one or two the following proteins or carbohydrates about 2-4oz (50g-110g) per person should be sufficient.

Proteins

Egg; poached or boiled
(the white part is highest in protein)
Meat; bacon or ham
Chicken, turkey
Cheeses; parmesan
low fat cheddar, cottage
Fish; tuna, mackerel,
smoked salmon, anchovy

Carbohydrates

potatoes, boiled
beans, haricot, flageolet
other white beans,
(freshly cooked or tinned)
croutons
toasted pitta pieces
avocados

Dressings

1. Classic Vinaigrette

These are the proportions for the classic vinaigrette which is made from olive oil and red wine vinegar. There is no reason why they cannot be applied to all the different combinations of oils and vinegars on the list. Try the same proportions but with different ingredients; walnut and balsamic vinaigrette, or hazelnut and lemon, or pumpkin and white wine.

If you wish to make larger quantities, just remember the basic proportions 1 part vinegar to 3 parts oil. Store them in a screw-top jar in the fridge. Remember oil and vinegar keeps indefinitely but the moment you add fresh herbs their life is shortened to about 3 days in the fridge.

Serves 4
Time, 2 minutes preparation

Ingredients
2tbs red wine vinegar
5tbs extra virgin olive oil
salt and pepper to taste

Equipment , tablespoon and screw top jar

Method
Put all the ingredients in a screw top jar and shake. This will keep indefinitely.

2. Herb and Mustard Dressing

This can be made with one or a combination of dressings. Add a touch of honey if you want it sweet or wholegrain mustard instead of Dijon - whatever takes your fancy.

Serves 4
Time, 4 minutes preparation

Ingredients
1tbs Dijon mustard
1 clove of garlic
1tsp honey
2tbs cider vinegar
5tbs virgin olive oil
2tbs of any of the following herbs; mint, chive, fennel, parsley, basil

Equipment - garlic press, sharp knife and chopping board, spoon, screw-top jar, blender

Method
1. Peel and chop the garlic finely or put it through the garlic press.
2. Put all of the ingredients into the blender and whizz so they are well combined.

3. Walnut Oil Dressing

To intensify the walnut taste, scatter a few walnuts over your salad. The sharpness of walnuts with a chalky goat's cheese, (or Roquefort) and rocket go particularly well (remember that the cheese is high in saturated fat). Walnuts are a good source of omega 3 oils which have anti inflammatory properties.

Serves 4
Time, 3 minutes preparation

Ingredients

2tbs Dijon mustard
3tbs red or white wine vinegar
7tbs walnut oil
salt and pepper to taste

Equipment, tablespoon and screw-top jar

Method

Put all of the ingredients in a screw-top jar and shake well.

Variation - Walnut and Basil Dressing

To make walnut and basil dressing put all of the ingredients in the blender along with six basil leaves and whizz. Remember that this will only keep in the fridge for about 3 days whilst the walnut dressing with mustard on its own will keep for about a week.

4. Raspberry and Crème Fraiche Dressing

This is delightfully fresh and fruity. Add a few fresh or frozen raspberries to enhance the flavour of the raspberry vinegar.

Serves 4
Time 4 minutes preparation

Ingredients

2tbs raspberry vinegar
8tbs olive oil
1tbs crème fraiche (reduced fat)
2 raspberries, mashed
black pepper
salt to taste

Equipment, spoon and screw-top jar

Method

Mash up the raspberries and the crème fraiche with a fork and then put all of the ingredients into a screw-top jar. Give a good shake until well combined. It will settle in the fridge when kept, shake it again before use.

Note: all fruits that stain your clothes contain antioxidant properties.

5. Low Fat Mayonnaise

This will reduce the fat content of mayonnaise by about half per spoonful. Use a supermarket 'light' mayonnaise and low fat, plain yoghurt. Remember the mixture will only last as long as the date on the yoghurt carton. Shop around for the lowest fat mayonnaise.

Serves 4
Time 3 minutes preparation

Ingredients
3tbs reduced fat mayonnaise
3tbs low fat yoghurt
1tbs lemon juice
salt and white pepper to taste

Equipment, spoon and screw-top jar

Method
Stir the two yoghurts together with a spoon and then add the lemon juice still stirring. If you want the mixture thinner but not sharper, just add a little milk.

Variation - Curried Mayonnaise
Mix one teaspoon of curry paste to the above low fat mayonnaise .

6. Sparky Citrus Dressing

Make this with either hazelnut or olive oil. They both taste good. To strengthen the lime flavour just grate a little of the zest into the dressing.

Serves 4
Time, 3 minutes preparation

Ingredients
5tbs hazelnut or olive oil
2tbs lime or lemon juice
pinch of sugar
1tbs grated zest of lime
salt and pepper

Equipment, spoon and screw-top jar

Method
Grate the zest of the lime and then squeeze 2 tbs of the juice into a screw-top jar. Combine the oil, sugar and seasoning and give a good shake.

Mixed Vegetable Salads - Tropical Salad

This is a substantial mixed salad. If you wish to turn it into a main meal, scatter cooked, peeled prawns or seafood over the finished salad. Allow 2-4 oz (50-110g) per person.

Serves 4
Time- preparation 12 minutes

Ingredients

8oz (225g) mixed green leaves
3 spring onions, chopped
1 small papaya
1 medium avocado
1 red pepper
juice of a lime
4tbs coriander, chopped
4tbs cashew nuts, unsalted, plain

Equipment – sharp knife and chopping board, mixing bowl, serving dish, spoon

Method

1. Combine the leaves, spring onions and coriander and arrange on a flat serving dish.
2. Peel and stone the avocado and cut it into chunks into a small bowl. Pour the lime juice over it making sure that it is completely coated to stop it turning brown.
3. Peel the papaya, cut it in half, scoup out the seeds and cut it into chunks. Add it to the avocado in the bowl.
4. Cut the red pepper in half, de-seed it and cut it into strips. Put it in the mixing bowl.
5. Make the Sparky Citrus Dressing and pour it into the bowl with the avocado, papaya and pepper. Toss and transfer and arrange over the salad leaves on the serving dish.
6. Roughly chop up the cashew nuts and sprinkle over the salad and serve.

Inside Knowledge
Mixed leaves contain fibre which is important for bowel health. Avocados contain vitamin E and healthy oils – they are not deserving of their reputation as being "fattening". Prevent oxidation by covering with citrus juice.

Grated Raw Beetroot with Lime Dressing, Goat's Cheese and Walnuts

This is a clean tasting nutritious salad. The walnuts and goat's cheese compliment the tastes perfectly.

Serves 4
Time, 10 minutes preparation

Ingredients

12oz (350g) raw beetroot, grated
12 walnut halves
4-6oz (110g-175g) goat's cheese
1 lime, grated zest
8tbs Sparky Citrus Dressing

Equipment - peeler, sharp knife and chopping board, grater, bowl for mixing, spoon

Method

1. Peel and grate about 1lb of raw beetroot in a bowl. This will give about 12oz of grated beetroot.
2. Make up the Sparky Citrus Dressing and mix up to 8tbs of it into the raw beetroot. Combine well.
3. Transfer to a serving dish and break the goat's cheese over the beetroot with the walnuts. Finish with grated zest of lime for the most wonderful colours.

Inside Knowledge
Beetroot contains useful minerals and is a good source of folic acid for which there is an increased requirement in pregnancy. Limes contain some bioflavinoids. Goat's cheese provides some protein although it is high in saturated fat. It is better tolerated by those who are sensitive to cows milk products. Walnuts contain omega 3 oils.

Banana and Cucumber Cream Salad

This is an unusual and delightfully creamy salad. Eat it with smoked salmon or cold meats for a full meal.

Serves 4
Time- 7 minutes preparation

Ingredients

2 bananas, medium, chopped
½ cucumber, peeled, chopped
6oz (175g) mixed salad leaves
5tbs reduced fat mayonnaise
5tbs low fat yoghurt
juice of a lemon
4tbs pumpkin seeds, ground

Equipment – sharp knife and chopping board, bowl for mixing, spoon, peeler, blender.

Method

1. Make up some ground pumpkin seeds. Put the seeds in the blender and whizz until coarsely ground. Transfer to a screw-top jar.
2. Combine the mayonnaise and yoghurt together in a bowl with the lemon juice retaining the thick, creamy consistency.
3. Peel and chop the cucumber and banana into the bowl and fold into the cream.
4. Arrange the green salad leaves on a serving dish and heap the cucumber and banana mixture on top, finishing with a sprinkling of ground pumpkin seeds.

Inside Knowledge
Most of the cucumber's nutrients are located in the skin, so if you are not going to peel it make sure it is washed thoroughly. Pumpkin seeds contain zinc and essential fats. They also provide some fibre. The banana is a good carbohydrate food and are a good source of Potassium so a useful post exercise food. The salad leaves are rich in fibre.

Aegean Tomato Salad

This simple salad has all the essence of an Aegean sunny day. Fresh oregano is best, but dried tastes good as well.

Serves 4
Time, 5 minutes preparation

Ingredients

4 tomatoes, large, ripe
3oz (75g) red onions, sliced
10 Kalamata olives
1tbs fresh oregano
2oz (50g) fresh rocket leaves
1tbs olive oil
1tbs red wine vinegar

Equipment – sharp knife and chopping board

Inside Knowledge
Tomatoes are high in lycopene which has been shown to have cardio and prostate protective properties. Onions belong to the same family as garlic and are good for gut health.

Method

1. Chop up the tomatoes, fresh oregano and slice the red onions.
2. Arrange the tomatoes on a plate with the rocket, and the onions. Sprinkle the oregano and kalamata olives. Pour over the olive oil and vinegar and add pepper to taste.

Raw Talent Shopping Check-list

Refer to this list every time you go shopping to make sure you have the necessary ingredients to make your salads.

Salad Leaves

Kos
Iceberg
Endive
Spinach
Lambs lettuce
Watercress
Rocket
Dandelion
Mustard and cress

Herbs

Chives
Parsley
Basil
Coriander
Fennel
Sorrel
Mint
Rosemary
Sage

Vegetables

Asparagus
Avocado
Green/orange/red/yellow peppers
Spring/red/white onions
Kalamata/green olives
Celery
Courgette
French Bean
Broad Bean
Tomatoes
Beetroot

Oils

Olive (cold first pressing)
Hazelnut
Pumpkin
Walnut
Sunflower (first pressed)
Rapeseed
Peanut
Linseed
Flaxseed

Vinegars

White/red wine
Cider
Balsamic
Sherry
Raspberry

Seeds and Nuts (raw unsalted)

Pumpkin
Sunflower
Sesame
Pistachio
Cumin
Pecan
Hazelnut
Cashew
Pine
Whole walnuts

Fruit

Raspberries
Pawpaw
Lime
Lemon
Banana

Miscellaneous

Dijon mustard
Crème fraiche
Yoghurt, plain low fat
Low fat mayonnaise
Goat's cheese

eating for energy

The following recipes are to provide some different choices for glycogen replenishment. Do remember that refined carbohydrates such as risotto rice are best used post exercise. Otherwise chose those foods that have not had any of their goodness removed such as brown rice, wholegrain pasta or pulses. In order to slow their release into the blood stream and provide muscle building fuel, you will need to add some protein such as chicken, turkey, fish, egg, or other lean meat. All of these recipes are easy and relatively quick to make.

Basic Tomato Sauce For Pasta, Risotto, Gnocchi and Polenta

A simple and versatile tomato sauce to accompany pasta, risotto, gnocchi or polenta. Make double or triple the quantities and store it in ordinary sized jam jars in the fridge for 2-3 days or alternatively put it in the freezer. Remember to leave the lid off when you freeze it because the sauce will expand by 10%. Replace the lid when fully frozen and make sure that it is labelled. To de-frost just take it out of the freezer until thawed or thaw gently in the microwave. Do not sink it into hot water or the glass will crack.

Serves 4
Time, 7 minutes preparation 15 minutes cooking
Sauce Freezes well

Ingredients
2tbs olive oil
8 oz (225g) chopped onion (a good sized onion)
2 x 400g tins of chopped tomatoes
4tsp tomato puree
2 cloves of garlic
1–2tbs fresh parsley or basil, chopped
salt and pepper to taste

Equipment – sharp knife, chopping board, can opener, medium pan (sauce) large, pan (pasta)

Method
1. Peel and chop the garlic, onion and parsley very finely and then fry them in a pan, stirring now and then until the onion turns clear and tender.
2. Stir in the tomato puree so that it is well combined with the onion and garlic and then add the tomatoes.
3. Transfer half to the blender and puree until smooth.
4. Return to the pan and bring to the boil. Immediately turn down the heat and simmer for 12 minutes with a lid on. Add the fresh herbs before serving.

Variation - Tomato and Tuna Sauce
For tomato and tuna sauce just add a tin of drained tuna (in brine not oil) after you have pureed the sauce. Put back on the heat, combine with the sauce and simmer for 12 minutes.

Inside Knowledge
Tomatoes contain lycopene an antioxidant that quenches free radicals. Onions, like garlic, have been shown to have antibacterial properties whilst olive oil is a good mono-unsaturated fat.

Penne With Fresh Mushrooms

Cook the pasta while you are making the sauce. If you have to cook pasta beforehand and keep it in the fridge, then it is best to use the individual shapes like penne or farfalle rather than spaghetti because it is less likely to stick. To minimise this toss in a tablespoon of olive oil just after cooking. Pasta, nevertheless is best cooked freshly.

Most supermarkets do mixed packs of interesting mushrooms such as Girolles, Paris Brown and Oyster. Otherwise use button mushrooms. Cepes would be wonderful with this recipe. Vegetarians need only miss out the bacon.

Allow about 3-4oz (90-110g) of pasta per person..

Serves 4
Time, 5 minutes preparation, 15 minutes cooking

Ingredients

12oz (350g) dried, cooked pasta
12oz (350g) fresh mushrooms
2tbs olive oil
4oz (110g) onion, finely chopped (a medium onion)
1 garlic clove
2 rashers lean back bacon
2oz (50g) grated Parmesan

Equipment – sharp knife, chopping board, medium pan for the sauce, large pan for the pasta, wooden spoon, grater

Method

1. Take the rind and the fat off the bacon. Chop the onion, garlic and bacon finely and fry them in a pan with the oil until tender and clear. Do not allow to burn.
2. Add the chopped mushrooms and cook for a few minutes until soft. You may have to turn up the heat if the mushrooms give off too much water.
3. On a medium heat, add the cooked pasta to the pan and heat through. Stir frequently.
Fold in the parsley and cheese. Adjust the seasoning.

Inside Knowledge
Certain mushrooms, particularly Shiitake have been shown in clinical trials to boost the immune system. Wholemeal spaghetti has a lower GI than white.

Gnocchi al Pomodoro

Gnocchi are small potato dumplings. Here they are served with tomato sauce for a quick and filling meal. If you need more protein, add 20z (50g) of peeled cooked prawns, per person and the dish becomes Gnocchi al Pescatore !

Serves 4
Time, 5 minutes preparation, 20 minutes cooking

Ingredients

10tbs of tomato sauce
Packet of gnocchi for four people.
8oz (225g) de-frosted prawns (optional)
2tbs of fresh herbs - basil or parsley
Parmesan, grated

Equipment – sharp knife, chopping board, grater, spoon, wooden spoon.

Method

1. Cook the gnocchi as per the instructions on the packet.
2. Drain them and return to the pan and add the tomato sauce.
3. Stir over the heat until properly warmed through and serve with freshly grated Parmesan.

Inside Knowledge
Processed tomatoes have high amounts of lycopene, a carotenoid which has antoxidant properties. White rice has a high GI.

Risotto With Three Herbs

Use Arborio rice for this - its distinctive creamy texture has a slight bite. For a starter you will need 2 oz (50g) rice per person and up to double that for a main course. Risotto and herbs go well together especially a mixture of chives, parsley and mint. Risotto benefits from a good stock and perhaps a dash of white wine. Like pasta it can be served in many ways and is best 'al dente'.

Serves 4 as a starter or 2 as a main course
Time, preparation 5 minutes, 20 minutes cooking

Ingredients

2tbs olive oil
1 medium onion, finely chopped
1 clove garlic
8oz (225g) Arborio rice, dry
1½ pts (900 mls) hot water or stock
1tbs each of parsley, chives and mint
salt and pepper
Parmesan, grated

Equipment – sharp knife and chopping board, large pan, grater, spoon and wooden spoon

Method

1. Wash and chop the herbs. Peel and chop the onion and garlic very finely. Fry them in a pan with the oil for a minute and then add the dry rice and continue frying for another two minutes, stirring continuously.
2. In another pan bring 1½ pts (900 mls) hot water or stock to the boil. Add the hot stock to the rice, one ladleful at a time until it is all absorbed. Simmer for a good 20 minutes, stirring most of the time and adding more stock if you have to.
3. Stir in the chopped herbs. Serve with grated Parmesan cheese.

Inside Knowledge
Using olive oil instead of butter reduces the saturated fat in this dish. Onions and garlic contain allicin which has been shown to reduce LDL (bad cholesterol).

Polenta

Polenta is maize meal. It is a staple food of the North of Italy. Like pasta and risotto it is versatile and used in a number of ways. You need to find 'quick cook' polenta or maize meal that is as fine as flour because it will cook quickly. It will easily sponge up ½ pt (275ml) of milk to every 2oz (50g) of meal and a little bit more so use semi-skimmed or skimmed milk to keep the fat down. Make it as you would custard, stirring all the time.

There are two ways of eating this polenta, either as you would porridge or in squares that have been cooked again in the oven. Both are given here and are served with the basic tomato sauce.

Serves 4
Time, 12-15 minutes cooking on the hob,
(20 minutes resting time) 10 minutes in the oven

Ingredients

6oz (175g) maize meal, very fine or instant
2pts semi-skimmed milk
1tsp salt
4oz (110g) Parmesan, grated
10tbs tomato sauce

For oven version
1 egg, beaten
2oz butter

Equipment non-stick pan, wooden spoon, baking tray or flat ovenproof dish, non-stick baking paper, knife, grater

Method

1. Put the maize meal in a non-stick pan and slowly add 1½ pts (825ml) of the warm milk stirring all the time so that there are no lumps.
2. Put it on the heat and make it as you would custard. When it has thickened, keep it on the hob for another seven minutes or so, to cook the maize through properly. Whilst this is happening you may need to add more milk, or water if you do not want any more fat. Taste it to make sure that it is properly cooked. By this stage it should be firm but not sloppy. Stir in the grated Parmesan.
3. You can at this point spoon the polenta into bowls, heat up some tomato sauce and eat it like porridge.
4. Alternatively if you are going out and want something quick and sustaining when you come in. Quickly stir a beaten egg into the mixture. Make sure it does not coagulate. Cook for another minute or two and then turn the mixture out onto non-stick baking paper placed over a flat oven dish or baking tray. Smooth it over with a spatula or knife and put it in the fridge for at least 20 minutes. (It will keep like this for a good 2 days, but cover it.)
5. When you want it, pre-heat the oven to a hot 220 c/ 425f/Gas mark 6.
6. Take the tray out of the fridge and cut it into 2" (5cm) squares. Arrange the squares on a well greased oven-proof dish and dot with butter.
7. Bake for 10-15 minutes until the squares are golden brown. Serve with tomato sauce.

Inside Knowledge
Polenta is a good alternative choice of carbohydrate, its flour is rich in carotenoids.

Eating for energy shopping check-list

Refer to this list every time you go shopping

Dry Goods
Wholewheat pasta (various)
Quick cook or very fine polenta
Arborio rice

Bottles and Tins
Olive oil
Tinned tomatoes
Tomato puree

Fresh Vegetables and Herbs
Onion
Mushrooms
Garlic
Parsley
Basil

Proteins
Bacon (lean back)
Parmesan cheese
Semi-skimmed milk
Peeled cooked, prawns

GILBERT
BTcellnet

winning main meals

This section gives ten low fat protein dishes and a choice of five carbohydrate and five vegetable dishes. Additionally there is information on how to cook and prepare other simple types of vegetables and carbohydrates to give many interesting combinations.

When eating for sport and general health, it is important to have a mixture of protein and carbohydrate in your main meal. To achieve this, mix and match the following menus to arrive at a healthy balance.

Carbohydrates

Main courses can be served with rice, noodles,lentils, pasta, polenta, potatoes or carbohydrate winter roots such as parsnip, sweet potato or Jerusalem artichoke.

Rice is perhaps the only one that needs specific instructions here. Four types of rice are recommended;

Basmati white or brown,
Wild rice which is in fact a grass,
Long grain brown rice,
Carmargue red rice.

For light fluffy rice first follow the directions on the packet. When the rice is cooked drain it through a sieve over the sink. Finish by pouring a kettle of boiling water over the rice. This washes out all the extra starch which makes it stick. Drain it well and serve, or put it in a low oven covered with foil to keep until the meal is ready.

For a short-cut make rice in batches and freeze it in plastic bags. When you wish to use it bring it out, defrost it in the microwave and then put it on high for a minute or two. (Seriously messed-up rice seems to magically right itself this way).

If you are cooking with coconut milk and have some left over add a few tablespoons to the rice water for an extra fragrancy. Alternatively, large cardamom pods added to the water make a pleasant change.

Polenta and pasta are covered in the Eating for Energy section. Potatoes simply boiled and then put through a ricer is a good source of carbohydrate. For plain noodles or lentils follow the directions on the packet.

Brown Rice Salad With Apricots

Serves 4
Time, preparation 10 minutes, rice 25 minutes

Ingredients

8oz(225 g) brown rice
1 yellow or red pepper
3oz (75g) dried apricots (about 8)
4 spring onions, finely chopped
3oz (75g) courgettes, chopped
2tbs fresh mint or coriander
2oz (50g) flaked almonds

Equipment – medium pan, serving bowl, sharp knife, chopping board

Method

1. Cook the brown rice as per the instructions on the packet. It will take about 25 minutes. Allow to cool or alternatively rinse through a sieve with cold water from the tap.
2. Meanwhile de-seed and chop the pepper. Chop the spring onions finely, the apricots into small chunks, the courgettes into batons and the fresh mint or coriander. Combine.
3. Serve with a dressing if you wish (See raw talent dressings) Alternatively you can heat it up in the microwave for a minute or so.

Inside Knowledge
Brown rice contains some B vitamins, and fibre. It is a complex carbohydrate with a higher GI than white spaghetti, but is nevertheless preferable to white rice. Dried apricots contain some iron whilst courgettes are a good fibre source. Red peppers contain more beta-carotene than the other colours and contain the natural pain killer capsaicin.

Orange Sweet Potato Mash (With Coconut Milk)

The coconut milk is optional but makes a delightful variation if you have some handy. Serve this with Tangy Orange Chicken.

Serves 4
Time, 6 minutes preparation, 20 minutes cooking
Freezes

Ingredients
2lb (900g) sweet potato
Orange juice, enough to cover the potato in the pan
2tbs coconut milk
salt and pepper to taste

Equipment – medium pan, masher (or food processor) peeler, sharp knife and chopping board

Method
1. Peel and chop the sweet potato into chunks.
2. Put it in a pan with enough orange juice to cover the potatoes and bring to the boil. Simmer for about 15-20 minutes or until tender.
3. Drain and reserve the orange juice. This is best put through the food processor if you have one as it tends to clog up in the blender. Otherwise mash by hand with a masher. To intensify the orange taste just add back some of the reserved orange juice. Alternatively stir in a few tablespoons of coconut milk to get the consistency you want.

Inside Knowledge
Sweet potatoes contain carotenes and other carotenoids. It has a low GI combined and with the coconut milk provides a good form of energy.

Brown Rice Bubble and Squeak

Make up a large amount of this, shape it into individual patties and freeze.
When you cook brown rice, just make a little extra and freeze it in a plastic bag for this recipe. Use potatoes that keep their shape, alternatively use left-over mashed potato.

Serves 4
Time, preparation 10 minutes, cooking 10-15 minutes.

Ingredients

12oz (350g) new potatoes in their skins
4oz (110g) cooked brown rice or just over 1oz (25g) dry
4oz (110g) leeks, chopped (one medium)
4tbs hummus
1tbs fresh parsley

Equipment – sharp knife and chopping board, masher or fork, bowl for mixing, frying pan

Inside Knowledge

Brown rice and new potatoes have a high GI whilst the chickpeas are low providing a mix of slow and quick release carbohydrates. The chickpeas and sesame seeds from the tahini provide the nutrients to make up a complete protein. They also provide some B vitamins.

Method

1. Either use left-over brown rice or put just over 1oz (25g) of rice in boiling water and follow instructions on the packet.
2. Wash and slice the potatoes. Put them in a pan of boiling water and a little salt and boil for 10-15 minutes.
3. Wash and finely slice the leeks and fry in a pan with the oil until they are tender and clear. Chop the parsley.
4. Drain the potatoes and mash with a fork in a bowl. Add the cooked brown rice, the leeks, the hummus, and the parsley. Combine well.
5. Shape into patties and fry in a little oil on a medium heat until golden brown on both sides.

Saffron Frumenty

Frumenty is the English medieval answer to cous cous. Here it is cooked as you would a risotto. Add some peas to it if you wish, or grate some parmesan.

Serves 4
Time, preparation 5 minutes,cooking 15-20 minutes

Ingredients

8oz (225g) cracked wheat
2pts (1.2 litres) chicken/vegetable stock
a few saffron strands
large onion, chopped
1 clove garlic
2tbs parsley, chopped
2tbs olive oil
2 egg yolks, beaten
salt and pepper to taste
grated Parmesan (optional)

Equipment – sharp knife and chopping board, fork and small mixing bowl, medium pan, grater

Method

1. Chop the onion and fry gently in the oil on a medium heat until tender and clear.
2. Add the cracked wheat, the saffron and the warm stock ladle by ladle. Bring to the boil and then simmer for a good 15 minutes. Leave to swell more if you wish. Chop the parsley and beat the eggs.
3. Drain off the excess moisture and add the beaten egg yolk stirring all the time until it has thickened. Do not allow to coagulate like scrambled egg. Toss in the parsley and adjust the seasoning. Serve on its own or with meat.

Inside Knowledge
Egg yolks are a good source of vitamin B12 and parsley is used by herbalists as a diuretic. Parsley, when chewed is said to control the odour of garlic.

Winter Vegetable Roast

Follow this recipe for roasting sweet potatoes, parsnips and Jerusalem artichokes. Add a red onion for colour and extra taste. For a citrus glaze add a juice of a lime and a tablespoon of soft brown sugar to the contents of the roasting pan once everything is cooked. Stir it around then add the vegetables back to coat them before serving.

Serves 4
Time, 4 minutes preparation, 20 minutes cooking

Ingredients

1½ - 2 lbs (700g-900g) winter vegetables
2-4 cloves of garlic
3tbs olive oil
pinch of dried mixed herbs

Equipment – peeler, spoon, knife, chopping board, flat oven proof dish

Method

1. Peel the sweet potato and dice it into ½" (1cm) chunks. Peel the parsnips and quarter them length-ways. Wash and peel the Jerusalem artichokes and chop them into about ½" (1cm) chunks. Peel and chop the garlic.
2. Put them in a flat oven proof dish with the oil.
3. Mix the oil and the vegetables so that all surfaces are lightly coated.
4. Roast in the oven at 200c/ 400f/Gas Mark 6 for 20 minutes or until crispy and cooked.

Inside Knowledge
Jerusalem artichokes are high in inulin which is a fructo-oligosaccharide. It is also a prebiotic and provides food for the good bacteria in the gut. Parsnips have a high GI, whilst sweet potatoes have a low GI.

Vegetables

Eat an abundance of vegetables, steamed, roasted, stir-fried or simply raw. If you are trying to reduce body fat choose those that grow above the ground in preferance to root vegetables (which include parsnips, potatoes, swedes, turnips, carrots). Remember to wash all vegetables well in a vegetable wash to remove pesticides.

Vegetable Stir-Fry Formulae

Stir fry vegetables are a quick and nourishing accompaniment to any of the protein recipes. Be creative. An interesting and balanced stir fry for four people would consist of four different vegetables of about 4oz (110g) each, perhaps more.

Choose any vegetables from the following list;
Baby sweetcorn, beansprouts, broccoli, mangetout, spring onions, red onions, green/orange/red/yellow peppers, carrots, broad beans, kale,courgette, pak choy, grated brussel sprouts, cabbage, asparagus, spinach, mushrooms, French beans.

Here are two basic stir-fries, Oriental or Mediterranean. All you need to do is choose the vegetables.

Serves 4
Time, preparation 15 minutes, cooking 4-5 minutes

Equipment –sharp knife and chopping board, wok, wooden spoon

Oriental Stir-Fry Formula

Use half sesame seed oil, half sunflower oil and fragrant herbs like coriander.

Ingredients

1tbs sesame seed oil
1tbs sunflower oil
1 clove garlic
1/2" (1cm) chopped ginger
4 types of vegetable, allowing 4 oz (110g) per person
4 spring onions
1-2tbs soy sauce
1-3tbs coriander, chopped
1tbs honey or maple syrup (optional)
1-2tbs flaked almonds

Method

1. Wash the vegetables in a vegetable wash of water with a tablespoon or two of inexpensive vinegar. Chop them to the shape you want. Peel and finely chop the garlic and the ginger.
2. Heat the wok on a medium to high heat. Put the oil, garlic and ginger into the wok and stir. First add the larger more substantial vegetables like peppers, broccoli, sweet corn, carrots, broad beans. After 2-3 minutes add the lighter vegetables like spring onions, bean-sprouts, kale, spinach. When cooked but still crisp add the soy sauce, the honey/maple syrup, the coriander and nuts. Stir until well combined and serve immediately. Accompany with rice, noodles and/or a protein dish.

Mediterranean Stir-fry Formula

The Mediterranean stir-fry is simpler but no less effective. The Mediterranean diet is full of olive oil, flavonoids and carotenes!

Ingredients

2tbs olive oil
1 clove garlic
4oz red onion
4-5 types vegetables x 4oz (110g) per person
2tbs mixed herbs; rosemary, thyme, chives, parsley

Method

1. Peel and finely chop the garlic. Peel and chop the red onion.
2. Wash the vegetables as above and chop to the shape you want.
3. Heat the wok on a medium to high heat and then put in the oil and garlic whilst stirring. Add the other vegetables and the herbs. Stir now and then until the vegetables are cooked but still crunchy, about 4 –5 minutes.

Inside Knowledge
Eat as many varieties as you can
Eat as many colours as you can
Eat them as many ways as you can
Eat them raw as well as cooked when you can

Efficient elimination of toxins and waste products is a cornerstone of health.
Good sources of anti-oxidants are found in the following vegetables : broccoli, brussel sprouts, cabbage, cauliflower, horseradish, kale, turnip - also provide fibre. Steam, stir-fry or add them to other dishes.

Sweet Pepper and Mangetout Stir-fry with Almonds

This is a colourful and easy dish to cook. You can always chop the vegetables beforehand and leave them in the fridge for a few hours in a plastic bag if you have to go out. However, they lose their vitamin content once cut so try to cook them straight away.

If you want to make this into a protein meal, cut up four chicken breasts in strips and fry them in a little oil. Keep them warm whilst you cook the vegetables and serve together.

Serves 4-6
Time, 15 minutes preparation, 7 minutes cooking

Ingredients

1 pack of sweet peppers (red/yellow/orange)

4oz (115g) mangetout
8 spring onions
4oz (110g) broccoli florettes
1-2 cloves of garlic
½ " (1cm) grated ginger
1tbs honey
1tbs sesame seed oil
1tbs sunflower oil
2tbs light soy sauce
1oz (25g) flaked almonds

Equipment- sharp knife and chopping board, wok, wooden spoon

Method

1. Wash the vegetables in fresh water with a few capfulls of inexpensive vinegar to get all the pesticides off.
2. Halve and de-seed the peppers and cut them into strips. Peel and chop the garlic and grate the ginger. Break up the broccoli into florettes. Trim the spring onions and chop them finely using the green tops too.
3. Heat up the wok and then put in both the oils. Throw in the garlic and the ginger and give it a stir. Add the peppers and the broccoli, cook for 2 minutes, then add the mangetout. Cook for another 3 minutes.
4. Finally, add the soy sauce and honey stirring well to combine. Toss in the nuts and spring onions and cook for another minute and serve.

Inside Knowledge
Broccoli is a star food. It helps the liver in many ways and is thought to protect against cancer. The grated ginger is good for the stomach whilst the almonds provide some minerals and a little protein.

Crunchy Vegetable Kebabs with Tofu

A good vegetarian dish as a vegetable accompaniment or main meal. If you do not have a store of ground nuts and seeds, put a few ounces of seeds/nuts into a blender and whizz until grainy. Transfer to a screw-top jar and store in the fridge for this and future use.

Serves 4-6
Time, 15 minutes preparation, 10 minutes cooking

Ingredients

10oz (300g) smoked tofu
12 cherry tomatoes
1 yellow/orange pepper
6oz (175g) button mushrooms
1 courgette
1 red onion
3tbs olive oil
juice of lime or lemon
1tbs parsley or chives, chopped
1oz (25g) seeds or nuts, finely ground
salt and pepper

Equipment - wooden kebab or satay sticks, sharp knife and chopping board, brush, small mixing bowl, spoon

Method

1. Chop the tofu into cubes. Peel the onion and quarter it lengthways. Halve the peppers lengthways, de-seed them and chop into cubes. Top and tail the courgette and cut it into slices. Put the grill on to medium.
2. Combine the lemon juice, the chopped parsley and olive oil into a small mixing bowl.
3. Thread the tofu and vegetables onto the sticks. Brush with the lemon juice mixture.
4. Put under the grill, turning and basting until they are golden brown.
5. Sprinkle the ground seeds/nuts onto a plate and roll the kebabs in it. Serve immediately.

Inside Knowledge
A good protein dish for vegetarians in the form of tofu and nuts. Vary the vegetables if you wish, but the peppers contain beta carotene and capsaicin which has anti inflammatory properties. Mushrooms contain some B vitamins. Onion contain an antioxidant called quercitin.

Carrot and Parsnip Puree

This is carrot and parsnip puree with a difference - if you like coconut milk.

Make this in advance and heat up in the oven or microwave. Dot with a little butter if using the oven which will take 15-20 minutes at 180c/ 350f/Gas Mark 4. If the microwave, cover with clingfilm and cook on high for about 3 minutes. Stir well to ensure even heat distribution. It will keep in the fridge for 2-3 days.

Serves 4
Time, preparation 10 minutes, cooking 10 minutes
Short-cut 6 minutes

Ingredients

10oz (275g) carrots
10oz (275g) parsnips
clove of garlic
good pinch cinnamon (optional)
1tbs parsley, chopped
4tbs milk or coconut milk

Equipment – peeler, sharp knife, chopping board, blender or potato masher, medium pan or microwaveable dish with non-pvc clingfilm

Method

1. Either bring a saucepan of salted water to the boil. Peel, trim and chop the parsnips, carrots and garlic and then add them to the water. Simmer for 10-12 minutes until tender.
2. Put the cooked vegetables in the food processor or mash them with a masher, until smooth. Add a few tablespoons of coconut milk to improve the consistency. Return to the heat if necessary. Stir in the cinnamon and garnish with fresh parsley.

Short cut

Or, peel, trim and chop the carrots and parsnips. Put into a microwaveable dish with a little water on the bottom. Cover with clingfilm and cook on high for about 6 minutes until tender.

Inside Knowledge
This dish is has a very high Glycaemic Index (both vegetables are in the 90s) so is good for glycogen (energy) replacement after training. Eat this with brown rice and meat or fish for slow release energy. Carrots are a rich source of beta carotene, particularly when cooked.

Garlic Stuffed Tomatoes

Easy to make and just as tasty cold, especially during the summer time.

Serves 4
Time, preparation 10 minutes, cooking 15 minutes

Ingredients

4 large tomatoes
2 cloves of garlic
8tbs breadcrumbs
2tbs parsley, chopped
2tbs basil, chopped
2tbs olive oil
4tbs Parmesan
salt and pepper to taste

Equipment – Sharp knife, chopping board, grater, garlic press, small bowl for mixing, ovenproof dish.

Method

1. Put the oven on to 180c/350f/Gas Mark 4.
2. Peel and put the garlic through a garlic press or chop very finely. Chop the basil and the parsley. Either get some breadcrumbs out of your stock in the freezer, or chop up a slice of brown bread into chunks and put it through the blender until it crumbs.
3. Cut the tomatoes in two, transversally. With a tea-spoon scoop out the pips and put them into a small bowl. Add the oil the parsley, basil, breadcrumbs and Parmesan and mix together. Put the mixture back into the tomatoes.
4. Arrange on an oven proof dish and bake for about 15 minutes or until the tomatoes are cooked but still firm.

Inside Knowledge
Tomatoes contain lycopene which is good for heart and prostate health as well as containing some vitamin E and beta carotene. Garlic has been shown to help reduce bad cholesterol well as having anti-bacterial, and anti-fungal properties.

The 'All-In' Omelette

An 'All-in' is military slang for putting the entire contents of everyone's ration pack into the one pan to make a complete meal. The method for this omelette, however, is based on the correct way to make a Spanish Tortilla which is to mix the hot potatoes in a separate bowl with the beaten egg before putting it back in the frying pan to finish off. Make this with left-over potatoes and cooked frozen peas. Size matters. You need an 8"(20) cm frying pan.

Serves 2
Time, 6 minutes preparation, 10 minutes cooking

Ingredients

4 eggs, beaten
1tbs olive oil
10oz (275g) left-over potatoes
6oz (175g) peas, cooked
1 large onion, sliced
salt and pepper to taste

Equipment – 8"/20cm, frying pan, sharp knife and chopping board, fork, wooden spatula, sieve, small pan

Method

1. If you do not have any left over peas in the fridge, put 6oz (175g) on to boil for five minutes, drain and reserve. Meanwhile finely chop the onion and slice the left-over potatoes.
2. Melt the oil in the frying pan and then add the onion. Fry on a medium heat until the onion is tender and clear. Do not brown.
3. Add the chopped potato and peas *and continue until they are heated through, stirring now and then. Season with a little salt and pepper.
4. Beat the eggs with a fork, in a separate bowl and then add the hot potatoes and peas and stir for a minute or two until well combined and the egg begins to coagulate. Return the mixture to the frying pan and continue to cook until the bottom of the mixture is golden.
5. Turn out onto a plate and cut it in slices as you would a cake.

*For variety, add a teaspoon of curry paste or powder to the mixture when you add the potatoes and peas. Make sure that it is well combined. Enjoy this with a Great Green or mixed salad.

Inside Knowledge
This is a complete meal with protein, carbohydrate and vegetables. To increase protein without fat, add two extra egg whites. The peas provide some fibre.

Protein Main Meals

Protein is a vital part of the sport person's diet, because it provides the building blocks for growth and repair of muscle. By adding protein to a meal, high GI elements such as potatoes and pasta, will have less effect on blood sugar levels.

Salmon Burgers

Use organic salmon which is less intensively farmed. Buy filleted, boned salmon. You may have to separate the skin from the flesh. Do this with a very sharp knife by pinching the salmon skin and sliding the knife as close to the skin as possible Push the knife down and away so that the skin separates from the flesh. Keep an eye out for the odd bone.

Serve this with stir- fry or roasted vegetables allowing 4-6oz (110g-175g) per person.

Serves 4
Time, 6 minutes preparation, 4 minutes cooking

Ingredients

12oz (350g) filleted, skinned salmon
4-6 spring onions, chopped
2 medium eggs, beaten
2-3tbs cottage cheese
2tbs parsley, chopped
1tsp lemon/lime juice
good pinch of paprika
salt and pepper to taste

Equipment – sharp knife and chopping board, fork, (or food processor) wok or frying pan

Method

1. If you have a food processor then combine all the ingredients together. If not, chop the filleted salmon, the spring onions and parsley as finely as you can. Put them all in a mixing bowl with the other ingredients and mash with a fork.

2. If the mixture is too sloppy add a few breadcrumbs from your stock in the freezer. 1-2 tablspoons should be sufficient. Shape into burgers.

3. Heat up the wok or frying pan, add the oil and fry until golden, about 2-3 minutes on both sides.

4. Either set-aside on a warm plate whilst you stir-fry the vegetables or take the roasted vegetables out of the oven and serve immediately.

Inside Knowledge

Salmon is an excellent source of protein and omega 3 oils which are anti inflammatory and cardio protective.

Ginger Grilled Duck

Remove the skins from the duck to lower the fat content of this dish to 5g of fat per 100g.This works just as well with chicken, which is lower in fat content.

Serves 4
Time, 7 minutes preparation (20 minutes marinade)
14 minutes cooking

Ingredients

4 good sized duck breasts
juice and zest of 1 lime
1" (2.5cms) of peeled ginger, finely grated
1clove garlic
2tbs soy sauce
1tbs honey
1tbs coriander

Equipment, grater, sharp knife and chopping board, shallow dish

Inside Knowledge
Duck is a good source of protein but relatively high in fat. Remove the skins and grill to reduce this.

Method

1. Grate the zest of the lime and squeeze the juice. Peel and grate the ginger. Peel and finely chop the garlic. Combine the zest, juice, ginger, soy, garlic and salt in a small bowl. Chop the coriander and set aside.
2. Remove the skin from the duck. With a very sharp knife, make deep criss-cross scores in the duck flesh and place in a shallow oven dish.
3. Brush the scored surface of the duck with the mixture and marinate for at least 20 minutes. (Meanwhile chop and prepare the vegetables for the stir-fry.)
4. Pre-heat the grill to high. Brush the marinated duck with the honey (warmed a little if too stiff) and cook for 7 minutes on each side, turning and basting or until the duck is cooked and slightly pink in the middle. Finish with the coriander and serve with stir-fry vegetables.

Chicken Kebabs With Yoghurt, Lemon and Garlic

This makes a deliciously tender kebab which can be cooked under the grill, in the oven or over the barbeque. Marinate the chicken for at least 20 minutes or better still, overnight.

Serve with rice and a salad.

Serves 4
Time 5 minutes preparation,
(20 minutes marinating) 14 minutes cooking

Ingredients
4 chicken breasts
2 cloves of garlic
juice of 2 lemons
1tbs olive oil
8tbs low fat bio yoghurt
1tbs fresh mint
1 red pepper
1 red onion
salt and pepper

Equipment – kebab sticks or skewers, sharp knife and chopping board, garlic press, bowl for marinating

Inside Knowledge
Chicken is an excellent source of low fat protein. It contains only 4g of fat per 100g. The bio yoghurt is good for intestinal flora and helps to maintain a healthy digestive system.

Method
1. Make the marinade by squeezing the lemon juice, chopping the mint and garlic and combining them with the yoghurt in a bowl with a little salt and pepper.
2. Cut the chicken up into bite sized chunks and add to the bowl. Marinate for at least 20 minutes.
3. Meanwhile chop the red pepper into chunks, and quarter the onion lengthways. (At this point put some rice on to boil or make a green salad).
4. Put the grill on high and place some foil at the base to catch the drips. Thread the chicken, the red pepper and slices of red onion onto the skewers. Grill, basting with the remaining marinade, turning frequently to avoid sticking for 10-15 minutes or until the centre of the chicken is properly cooked.

Tangy Orange Chicken With Thyme

Cook in a frying pan, or a wok and serve with rice or noodles and stir-fry vegetables. Do not miss out the thyme. Add a little cornflour to the sauce if you like it thicker.

Serves 4
Time 5 minutes preparation, 12 minutes cooking time

Ingredients

4 chicken breasts
4-5fl oz (150ml) orange juice
juice of one lemon
2 cloves of garlic
1tbs fresh thyme (or 1 tsp dried)
2tbs olive oil

Equipment – frying pan or wok, sharp knife and chopping board, warmed plate

Method

1. Fry the chicken breasts whole with 1tbs of olive oil for about 10-12 minutes or until cooked in the middle.
2. Meanwhile chop the thyme and garlic, grate the lemon zest and squeeze the juice.
3. Remove the cooked chicken from the pan on to a warm plate.
4. Pour the orange juice, lemon juice, zest, thyme and remaining oil into the pan and turn the heat up so that it bubbles. Stirring all the time allow the sauce to reduce by at least half. Put the chicken back to re-heat and serve immediately.

Inside Knowledge
Thyme has antioxidant properties. Chicken is a good source of low fat protein. Lemon contains bioflavonoids, and vitamin C although much of this is destroyed by cooking.

Chicken with Garlic Sauce

You have to eat this with something that is going to mop up the garlic sauce - like mashed potato. To avoid adding fat to the potato use a potato ricer. Accompany with steamed spinach and a squeeze of lemon.

Serves 4
Time, 4 minutes preparation, cooking 25 minutes

Ingredients

4 chicken breasts, 4oz-5oz (150g)
2tbs olive oil
1 head of garlic, unpeeled
1/2pt (300ml) dry white wine
1tbs fresh rosemary (1tsp dried)
3 sage leaves
salt and pepper

Equipment – frying pan with lid, warmed serving dish, potato masher or ricer

Method

1. Break up the head of garlic into individual cloves. Do not peel.
2. Heat a frying pan and add the oil. Put the chicken breasts and the garlic cloves in and brown for 5 minutes.
3. Add the wine and the herbs. Put a lid on the pan, turn the heat down and simmer gently for 15-20 minutes. When cooked transfer the chicken to a warm serving dish.
4. Mash the garlic into the sauce with a masher or fork. Adjust the seasoning.
5. Return the chicken to the pan with the sauce, re-heat and serve.

Inside Knowledge
Even when cooked garlic is good for you especially for cardiac health the reduction of bad cholesterol and possibly with the elimination of toxic metals. Spinach is a useful vegetable and contains beta carotene and carotenoid lutein, but it is high in oxalic acid which hinders the absorption of calcium and iron.

Beef Strips In Black Pepper

Ring the changes with different vegetables for this, try baby sweetcorn and broccoli or carrot and green pepper. Serve this with fragrant rice by adding coconut milk and a large cardamom to the water.

Serves 4
Time, 15 minutes preparation, 15 minutes cooking

Ingredients

2tbs sunflower oil
2-6 spring onions
1 lb (500g) organic fillet steak
2tbs honey or maple syrup
2tbs soy sauce
2tbs oyster sauce
2tsp black peppercorns
5oz (150g) mangetout
9oz (250g) mushrooms

Equipment – sharp knife and chopping board, pestle and mortar (or plastic bag and rolling pin), wok, wooden spatula, warm plate

Method

1. Chop the vegetables before the meat on the chopping board or you will have to wash it twice. First slice the mushrooms, and spring onion then slice the beef into thin strips. Crush the black pepper either in a pestle and mortar or put them in a plastic bag and crush them with a rolling pin.
2. You will need to fry the beef in batches - too many pieces together create water in the pan. Heat the wok on a high heat until hot. Add 1 Tbs of oil and carefully swirl it around the pan. Fry each batch for 3-4 minutes stirring all the time. Remove and drain on a double thick paper towel. Bring the wok back up to temperature and repeat. Transfer to a warm serving dish.
3. Add the remaining oil and stir fry the spring onions, mushrooms and mangetout. Transfer to the serving dish.
4. Add the honey, soy sauce, oyster sauce and pepper to the pan. Bring to the boil, reduce the heat and simmer for a few minutes until it has reduced a little.
5. Turn the heat up and return all the ingredients to the pan to heat through.

Inside Knowledge
Beef is a good source of protein but is higher in fat than most, even when lean. If you can source free range it will be leaner. Red meat is a good source of iron so is a useful inclusion in the diet once or twice a week.

Baked Sea Bass With Mint and Olive Oil

Fresh Sea Bass is best cooked simply. Always line foil baked dishes with non-stick baking paper as aluminium leaches into the food from the foil. Any fish is suitable for this method of cooking, try salmon or cod with herb butter instead of olive oil. Serve with boiled new potatoes and a few French beans.

Serves 4
Time 5 minutes preparation, 15 minutes cooking

Ingredients

4pieces of Sea Bass 5-6oz (150g) each
2tbs olive oil
4tbs orange juice
4 large sprigs of mint
salt and pepper

Method

1. Pre-heat the oven to 190c/ 375f / Gas 5. Put the orange juice and olive oil in a small bowl with a little salt and pepper and mix.
2. Cut out four 12"(30cm) squares of non-stick baking paper and the same of foil. Put a square of foil on the bottom and baking paper on top and then one piece of fish in the middle. Do this for each piece of fish.
3. Place a sprig of mint on each piece of fish and spoon the oil and wine mixture over equally. Shape into parcels taking care not to tear the foil and place on a shallow baking tray.
4. Bake in the oven for 15 minutes or until the fish is 'just' firm. Serve immediately.

Inside Knowledge
Sea bass is an excellent form of low fat protein and is easy on the digestion cooked this way with mint and olive oil. Mint is kind to the stomach because it contains anti-spasmodic volatile oils such as menthol which is used by herbalists to calm the intestines. Olive oil is a good source of mono-unsaturates.

Lamb Souvlakia

This dish benefits from marinating to make it deliciously tender. Shoulder fillet is marbled with fat and it is important that most of it is cut off. The enzyme action from the lemons tenderises the meat, which might otherwise be tough. Serve this with warm wholemeal pitta bread and a chunky Aegean Salad.

Serves 4
Time, 10 minutes preparation (overnight refrigeration) 12 minutes cooking

Ingredients

2lbs (1kg) lamb fillet
4fl oz (120mls) olive oil
4fl oz (120mls) lemon juice
2 cloves garlic, crushed
3tsp dried oregano leaves
1 red pepper
1 green pepper
a little salt and pepper

Equipment – kebab sticks or skewers, sharp knife and chopping board, bowl for marinating, clingfilm

Method

1. Trim the lamb of excess fat and sinew and cut into 1½ (3cm) cubes.
2. Peel and chop the garlic, mix the oil, lemon juice, oregano, garlic and seasoning in a bowl and then put the cubes of meat into it. Cover with cling film and rest in the fridge overnight. (see short-cut)
3. Put the grill on to medium.
4. Take the meat out, drain and keep the marinade.
5. De-seed and chop the peppers into 1½" (3 cm) squares.
6. Thread the meat and peppers alternately onto the skewers and grill for about 10 minutes, basting regularly and turning.

Short Cut

Buy-in double the amount of lamb, and when you have a spare moment cube it and make the marinade. Batch and store in the freezer for up to a month in airtight containers. On the day that you require it, remove it from the freezer and let it stand at room temperature to defrost for a few hours - it will de-frost and marinate at the same time. You then only have to grill it.

Inside Knowledge
Lamb is usually reared non-intensively and is therefore a good choice. Fillet is lower in fat than other cuts and a good source of iron.
The lemon juice will provide small amounts of bioflavonoids in these quantities.

Roast Salmon with A Pistachio Crust

This recipe can be adapted to other varieties of fish including cod and plaice.

Serves 4
Time 7 minutes preparation, 15 minutes cooking

Ingredients

4 x salmon fillets, 6oz (175g) each
3oz (75g) pistachio nuts, shelled, unsalted
juice and grated rind of 1 lemon
4 spring onions
4oz (110g) brown breadcrumbs
2oz (50g) lean back bacon
2tbs fresh parsley
2oz (50g) butter, softened
2-3 ready to eat dried apricots

Method

1. Put the oven on to 200c/400f/Gas Mark 6.
2. Put 3oz (75g) of natural, shelled pistachio nuts in the blender and grind to a rough powder.
3. Finely grate then juice the lemon and chop the parsley and apricots.
4. Chop the bacon finely and fry it in the pan with a little of the butter until it is cooked through. Chop the spring onions and then add them and the remaining butter, pistachio nuts, lemon rind, juice,apricots and breadcrumbs. Fry until golden stirring all the time.
5. Put some non-stick grease-proof paper on the base of a roasting dish and place the salmon on top. Spread the breadcrumb mixture over the salmon and pat it down so it is covered. Roast for 10-15 minutes until the salmon is 'just' done.

Inside Knowledge
Salmon is a good source of protein which is required for new muscle maintenance and growth. It also contains the omega 3 fatty acid, which is anti inflammatory and cardio protective. The pistachio nuts are an added source of protein whilst the breadcrumbs provide a small amount of vitamin B.

sweet success

Most of the sweets given here contain fruit. Use organic sugars or honey in preference to refined white sugar. If trying to lose body fat remember that the closer to the equator the fruit is grown, the higher the sugar content.

Pesche al Forno

Make with apricots if peaches are not available - just double the number because they are half the size.

Serves 4
Time, preparation 5 minutes, cooking 20 minutes

Ingredients

4 yellow peaches or nectarines
3oz (75g) crushed Amaretti or digestive biscuits
2tbs soft brown sugar
1 egg yolk
1oz (25g) butter
5fl oz (150mls) orange juice
1oz (25g) flaked almonds

Equipment, sharp knife, spoon, small mixing bowl, measuring jug, shallow ovenproof dish

Method

1. Put the oven on to 180c/ 350f/Gas Mark 4.
2. Rinse and dry the peaches, cut them in two and remove the stones. Arrange the 8 halves in a shallow ovenproof dish.
3. Crush the amaretti or digestives in a plastic bag and a rolling pin. In a small bowl, mix together the crushed biscuits, the sugar, egg yolk, and flaked almonds. Spoon the filling into the peach halves and pour the orange juice into the dish. Bake in a moderate oven for about 20 minutes. Serve warm or cold. Accompany with Greek or low fat yoghurt.

Inside Knowledge
Peaches contain some fibre and vitamin C. Vitamin C in the orange juice is destroyed when heated. Almonds provide a little protein, calcium and magnesium.

Millet and Walnut Biscuits

A good snack for those who cannot tolerate wheat.

Time 5 minutes preparation, 15 minutes cooking

Ingredients

4oz (110g) millet flakes
2tbs runny honey
2tbs vegetable or sunflower oil
1 egg, beaten
2oz (50g) walnuts, ground

Equipment - Baking tin, non-stick baking paper, mixing bowl, knife, wire rack

Method

1. Put the oven on to 180c/350f/ Gas mark 4.
2. Put the walnuts into the blender and whizz until powder.
3. Mix all the ingredients together in a bowl.
4. Shape into 9 cookies, about 2" (6cms) across. Bake for 15-17 minutes on a well oiled baking tray. Cool on a wire rack

Inside Knowledge
Millet is a good alternative carbohydrate to wheat. It contains B vitamins, phosphorus, some calcium and iron. It is gluten free and therefore useful for those who cannot tolerate wheat or gluten. The walnuts provide some protein.

Coconut and Banana Cream with Papaya

Use this quick and easy cream to fill a papaya. It takes a few minutes to mix so prepare it just before you need it as the banana discolours quickly.

Serves 4
Time, 5 minutes preparation

Ingredients
2 small papayas
2 bananas
zest of 1 lime
juice of $^1/_2$ lime
2-3tbs low fat Greek or bio yoghurt
2tbs coconut milk
1tbs dessicated coconut flakes
4 sprigs of mint

Equipment – sharp knife, chopping board, small mixing bowl, grater, teaspoon, blender

Inside Knowledge
Papaya contains papain which is a digestive enzyme. It is rich in beta-carotene and soluble fibre. Bananas are a good source of fibre, and potassium. The coconut milk contains some calcium and magnesium.

Method
1. Grate the zest and juice the lime.
2. Cut the papayas in half, lengthways and scoop out the seeds with a teaspoon. Place them on individual plates.
3. Mash the bananas with a fork in a small mixing bowl and pour in the lime juice and grated zest so they keep their colour and do not oxidise.
4. Stir in the dessicated coconut, the coconut milk and the yoghurt. Fill the four papaya halves and serve at once.

Baked Bananas

Easy to prepare well beforehand, but peel the bananas and cook them just as you need them or they discolour. Open the parcel out at the table and serve with crème fraiche or low fat fromage frais. If passion fruit are not available add an alternative, like peaches.

Serves 4
Time, 12 minutes preparation, 20 minutes cooking

Ingredients

4 bananas
4 passion fruit
8tbs orange or apple juice
2tbs honey (or soft brown sugar)
1oz (25g) butter
1tsp sesame seeds

Equipment – baking paper, aluminium foil, sharp knife, spoon, wooden spoon, small pan

Inside Knowledge
Bananas contain fibre and potassium whilst the passion fruits are a good source of carotenoids. Sesame seeds provide some magnesium, calcium and zinc.

Method

1. Preheat the oven to 180c/350f/Gas Mark 4. Line a shallow baking dish with foil on the bottom then baking paper on top.
2. Arrange the bananas on the baking paper. Scoop out the contents of the passion fruits and spoon them over the bananas with the honey/sugar and juice. Sprinkle the sesame seeds
3. Fold the baking paper and foil over the bananas to make a large parcel and bake for about 20 minutes until tender.
4. Open out the parcel at the table and serve with crème fraiche.

Strawberries with Balsamic Vinegar

Fresh ripe, strawberries in balsamic vinegar is very Italian and is served with freshly ground black pepper! Balsamic vinegars vary enormously. The best are those that have aged slowly and turned syrupy.

Serves 4
Time, 5 minutes preparation

Ingredients

2½ fl oz (70mls) lemon juice
1-2tbs caster sugar
1tbs balsamic vinegar
1lb (475g) fresh strawberries
black pepper

Equipment - bowl, two tablespoons, sharp knife, chopping board.

Method

1. Squeeze the lemon juice into a bowl, and add the sugar, stirring until it has dissolved then stir in the balsamic vinegars so that it makes a syrup.

2. Hull and halve the strawberries and toss them in the mixture as you would a salad. Serve with some fresh mint and a twist of black pepper.

Inside Knowledge
Strawberries contain flavonoids, and vitamin C. Flavonoids help prevent inflammation. Anti-oxidants can slow down the ageing process.

Warm Berries with Crème de Cassis

Crème de Cassis is a blackcurrant liqueur from Dijon and can be found in most supermarkets. Used here, it enhances the warmed black and red currants. The alcohol is killed off during cooking.

Serves 4
Time 5 minutes preparation, 5 minutes cooking

Ingredients

12oz (350g) blackcurrants, fresh or frozen
8oz (225g) redcurrants, fresh or frozen
rind and juice of 1 orange
4tbs caster sugar
low fat fromage frais
4tbs Crème de Cassis

Equipment – grater, small bowl, teaspoon, medium pan, sieve, serving dish, wooden spoon.

Method

1. Remove the red and black currants from their stalks. Grate the zest of the orange and then juice it.
2. Put the caster sugar, Creme de Cassis, orange juice, and zest in a pan and over a low-medium heat stir until the sugar has dissolved and the liquid reduced. Add the currants and bring up to the boil. Immediately turn down the heat and simmer gently for about 5 minutes.
3. Serve with crème fraiche or low fat fromage frais.

Inside Knowledge
Berries contain a good mix of flavonoids and anti-oxidants which can slow down the ageing process.

Raspberry and Rosewater Soup

Use this stunningly scented fruit soup to float fruit, mint or iced yoghurt. Do not miss out the rosewater which gives it its character. Buy rosewater in the baking section of the supermarket or at the chemist. If raspberries are not available use strawberries as an alternative.

Serves 4
Preparation 4 minutes

Ingredients

12oz (350g) raspberries, fresh or frozen
8fl oz (280mls) apple juice
4tbs rosewater
1-2 tsp honey

Equipment - measuring jug, blender, tablespoon.

Method

1. Put all of the ingredients in the blender, except the honey and liquidise until smooth.
2. Taste and then add one teaspoon of honey/sugar and taste again, repeat if necessary. (It needs to be sharp and sweet).
3. Float mint, chunks of fruit, yoghurt or low fat ice cream.

Inside Knowledge
Berries contain a good mix or flavonoids and anti-oxidants which are good for immunity and circulatory health.

Chilled Yoghurt Mousse

Enjoy this mousse plain or with fruit. Freeze it for a maximum of $1\frac{1}{2}$ hours so that it is chilled but not frozen.

Serves 4
Time, 7 minutes preparation, freeze up to 1 hour 30 minutes

Ingredients

6oz raspberries
12 heaped tbs low fat Greek yoghurt
6tbs runny honey
3 egg whites, whipped

Equipment – fork, bowl for raspberries, bowl for egg whites, whisk.

Inside Knowledge
Egg whites are a good source of low fat protein. Yoghurt is good for maintaining intestinal health.

Method

1. Mash the raspberries in a bowl with the yoghurt and honey.
2. Separate the eggs and whip the whites until they form soft peaks.
3. Carefully fold in the whipped egg whites into the raspberry mixture.
4. Put in the freezer, stirring now and then for about one hour 30 minutes until well chilled but not frozen.

A low fat alternative to whipped cream
Combine 4 heaped tablespoons of yoghurt and 2 tablespoons of runny honey to one beaten egg white. Freeze for about 1 hour 30 minutes and use as you would whipped cream.

LBERT

power drinks

All you need is a blender – minimum clearing up !

Power Drinks are the ultimate convenience food. Made in minutes, they deliver nutrition in a form which can be quickly digested and absorbed.

Power Drinks deliver power in many forms;
The Power of Recovery. Sugary carbohydrates are excellent post training. The insulin burst they provoke quickly replaces carbohydrates used through exercise.

The Power to Nourish. Power Drinks make a nutritious alternative to processed snacks. The fine oats in Breakfast in a Glass plus "Elite" protein will slow the release of sugars from the fruit and juices. Protein Power Drinks are useful pre-training especially when there is insufficient time to make or digest a meal.

The Power to reduce symptoms of Colds or Flu. Take 'A Row All To Yourself' contains high doses of garlic which has powerful anti-bacterial and anti-viral properties. Power Drinks with fresh orange juice, black-currants and berries all contain high amounts of vitamin C and other antioxidants which may help to prevent colds.

The Power to help Detoxify. Ready, Steady GO is made with prunes which are famous for their cleansing qualities. Fruit in the diet helps to cleanse the body and maintain regular bowel movements.

The Power to Balance. Ginger and mint can help to restore the stomach after upset or excess, whilst Power Drinks with oats and orange juice may help reduce and stabilise cholesterol levels. A Row All To Yourself contains garlic, which has been shown to reduce cholesterol.

Create Your Own Power Drinks Using These Formulae.

The Simple Power Drink is ideal for quick recovery after endurance training.

4oz fresh fruit **dried or frozen**	+	**8 fl oz fruit juice**	+	**4-6tbs low fat yoghurt** **or coconut milk**	**= Simple Power Drink**

The Compound Power Drinks are more of a complete meal and can be used after heavy training, or as a snack on the go

4oz fresh fruit **dried or frozen**	+	**9-10 fl oz fruit juice** **or skimmed milk, or low fat yoghurt, 2 scoops protein powder**	+	**1-2oz fine oats**	**= Compound Power Drink**

Keep a running supply of fresh, frozen or dried fruits, tomato juice, garlic, yoghurt, ground almonds and cocoa powder so you can make one when you need to.

Power drinks are good whoever you are! ... James, Flora, Nicholas and Miranda

Banana Colada

This is a non-alcoholic banana and pineapple version of the Pinacolada.

Serves one

Ingredients
2oz (50g) pineapple, chopped
2oz (50g) banana, chopped
8fl oz (200mls) apple juice
3tbs coconut milk

Method
1. Cut up the pineapple into small chunks having removed the skin and the core first. Chop up the banana.
2. Put all the ingredients in the blender and whizz until smooth and creamy.
Note; Banana discolours after about 15 minutes so if you wish to keep this drink looking creamy for longer add some fresh lemon juice.

Tip
If you have bananas that are ripening too quickly and you will not use them in time, just put them in the deep freeze and bring them out for this power drink – freezing makes them taste more creamy!

Inside Knowledge
Bananas contain potassium, and fibre. The banana has a high GI. Pineapple contains some vitamin C. It is rich in bromelain which aids digestion. The fat from coconut milk is a medium chain triglyceride, which is a useful source of fuel for athletes.

A Row All To Yourself – a garlic cure for flu

Try and buy good, plump succulent garlic. Take this at the first sign of a cold or if you have been mixing with anyone who has 'flu. Taking large quantities of garlic may marginalise you for a day or two, but so will staying in bed. Chew a little fresh mint or parsley to freshen the breath.

Serves One

Ingredients
3 cloves of fresh garlic
10fl oz (275mls) of tomato juice or V8
Good dash of Worcestershire sauce
Juice of a lemon
Good pinch of celery salt (optional)

Method
1. Put the garlic through a garlic press if you have one, or alternatively chop it up very finely.
2. Put it into the blender with a very small amount of tomato juice, the Worcestershire sauce, and the lemon. Whizz until the garlic is well combined with the juice (if you put in too much liquid the garlic stays lumpy). Add the rest of the tomato juice and give one blast to combine all ingredients. Serve.

Inside Knowledge
Garlic has many beneficial properties. It is anti-bacterial, anti-fungal, and has been shown to help protect against heart disease. The real issue however, is its smell.

The Cream of Hot Chocolates

A wonderfully warming and soothing chocolate drink for cold winter nights. For a treat serve with a stick of cinnamon.

Serves one

Ingredients

1½ oz (40g) ground almonds
½ pt (275mls) Milk (skimmed, semi-skimmed or soya)
Heaped teaspoon of best quality organic cocoa powder
Good pinch or cinnamon or vanilla essence
1 tsp honey if desired

Method

1. Put the almonds and the cocoa in a non-stick pan and stir in the milk slowly so that it is well combined . Bring to the boil and simmer gently stirring all the time for 5 minutes until the almonds thicken. (just like making custard)
2. Allow to cool for a minute or so, then pour in the blender and whizz for a good 15 seconds until the almonds are smooth and creamy.
3. Return to the heat if drinking immediately, sweeten and serve in a mug with a stick of cinnamon. Alternatively allow to cool and store in the fridge for 2-3 days. Re-heat when required.

Inside Knowledge
All nuts contain some minerals, protein and good oils. Soya contains phytoestrogens, especially genistein - shown to have a protective effect against breast and prostrate cancer.

Breakfast in a Glass - Creamy Fruit Oats and Yoghurt - for a complete meal

Have this for breakfast and you can spend an extra ten minutes in bed. Breakfast in a Glass is drinkable muesli. Made in a minute, it provides sustained energy and nutrition – brilliant if you are pressed for time. Add two scoops of protein powder to make this into a complete meal. Make with any fruit. Ideal before work or training, and will boost and sustain your blood sugar levels.

Buy the finely ground organic oatmeal. If not put ordinary oats in the blender (make sure it is absolutely dry) and whizz until finely ground. Store in a screw-top jar for further use. Alternatively use Quinoa flakes as a good source of protein.

Serves One

Ingredients

4 oz (110g) any fruit, fresh, dried, frozen
9 fl oz (275mls) apple or orange juice
1-2oz (50g) oats, finely ground
3 Tbs low fat bio yoghurt

Method

Blend all of the ingredients in the liquidiser until smooth and creamy. Pour and enjoy.

Inside Knowledge
Oats are a great source of soluable dietary fibre which can help lower blood cholesterol. Having a low GI they also provide slow releasing energy. Live yoghurt is good for maintaining intestinal health.

Creamapple Pine with Mint

The blended mint gives this an exhilarating dimension. Take care to stir the juice in to the yoghurt so that it keeps thick and creamy.

Serves one

Ingredients
2oz (50g) fresh pineapple, chopped
4fl oz (100mls) apple juice,
a good sprig of fresh mint
4tbs fat free plain yoghurt or low fat bio yoghurt

Method
1. Cut up the fresh pineapple into small chunks having removed the skin and core first.
2. Put the pineapple, apple juice and the fresh mint into the blender and give it a good whizz until the pineapple becomes pulp.
3. Spoon the yoghurt into a glass and then pour in the blended juice, stirring all the time so that it combines smoothly and does not become lumpy.

Inside Knowledge
This is good for digestion. The mint contains menthol which is good for indigestion, the pineapple contains bromelain which aids digestion. Live Yoghurt contains friendly bacteria which are good for bowel health.

A Date with Rose

Rosewater gives this drink the most exquisite fragrance. If unavailable, substitute two drops of vanilla or almond essence instead. Rosewater can be found in the cake-making section of any supermarket and, if not, the chemist.

Serves One

Ingredients
1oz (25g) fresh, pitted dates
1oz (25g) ground almonds,
5fl oz milk (150mls) skimmed or semi-skimmed or soya
1tbs of rosewater (or a few drops of vanilla essence)

Method
1. Pit and chop the dates quite finely. Put them into the blender with the almonds, rosewater or vanilla and milk.
2. Blend for a good fifteen seconds until smooth and creamy then serve. Do not add sugar, the dates make it sweet enough.
3. This can be kept in a fridge for 2-3 days. It will settle after a while, so give it a good stir before serving again.

Inside Knowledge
Dates are a good source of dietary fibre although very high in sugar. They also contain some potassium. Almonds contain some minerals a little protein and good oils.

Ready, Steady, GO ! – the cleansing power of prunes

Prunes have always been known for their cleansing properties! Try the same recipe with apricots – which are full of iron. This is just as good for pregnant women as sportsmen.

Serves One

Ingredients
4oz (110g) stoned, ready to eat prunes (or apricots)
11fl oz (275mls) orange juice
Pinch of cinnamon (optional)

Method
1. Chop up the prunes quite finely.
2. Blend all of the ingredients in a liquidiser until smooth.
3. This will keep in the fridge for 2-3 days, but you may need to add more apple juice because the dried fruit swells a little over time.

Inside Knowledge
Prunes have a natural laxative effect. They are a good source of fibre, and iron.

Cold Comfort – hot blackcurrant

A hot blackcurrant, rich in vitamin C is especially comforting when nursing a cold or after exertion in the freezing rain.

Serves One

Ingredients
4oz (110g) blackcurrants, fresh or frozen
10 fl oz (275mls) orange juice
1 clove (optional)

Method
1. Simmer the blackcurrants in half the orange juice with the clove for 10 minutes on a low heat. Mash them a little with a masher or fork when they are soft to get the best of the juice.
2. Pass them through a strainer, pressing down to be sure to get all the juice out.
3. Add the remaining orange juice. Serve with a sprig of mint.

Inside Knowledge
Blackcurrants are a good source of vitamin C. Use fresh orange juice but do not heat it all up as heat destroys the vitamin C. Use it as part of a cholesterol reducing diet. Cloves have some antiseptic properties. Fruits that stain clothes are a good source of antioxidants.

B'ango – banana and mango smoothie

The banana will oxidise and discolour after a while. If you want to preserve its colour, then add an acid like lemon juice.

Serves One

Ingredients
2oz (50g) banana,
2oz (50g) mango,
4fl oz (100mls) pineapple juice,
4tbs low fat bio yoghurt or low fat plain yoghurt

Method
1. Peel and chop the mango. Chop up the banana. Put them both in the blender with the apple juice. Whizz until smooth.
2. Spoon the yoghurt into a glass and add the blended juice to it, stirring all the time so that it remains thick and smooth.

Inside Knowledge
Banana contains potassium, and fibre. Pineapple contains bromelain, a digestive aid. It contains some vitamin C. The live yoghurt provides some friendly bacteria to maintain intestinal health and the mango is rich in carotenoids and soluble fibre which is great for bowel health.

Perry Berry Good

Make this with one or a mixture of berries including; raspberries, blueberries, tayberries, blackcurrants, redcurrants or strawberries.

Serves One

Ingredients
4oz (110g) fresh or frozen berries
6fl oz (150mls) apple or orange juice
3tbs low fat plain or bio yoghurt
Honey to taste

Method
1. Put the berries and juice in the blender and whizz until smooth.
2. Spoon the yoghurt into a glass and add the juice to it stirring all the time so that it is smooth and thick.
3. If it is too sharp, add a little honey.

Inside Knowledge
Berries contain a good mixture of flavonoids. As well as being anti-oxidants, flavonoids are good for circulatory health. Ant-oxidants may help slow down the ageing process. Live yoghurt contains good bacteria that can help maintain intestinal health; the bacteria support immunity.

Index

Soups

Snacks

Salads and raw vegetables

Main meals

Carbohydrate meals or accompaniments

Vegetable accompaniments

Sweets

Power drinks

Anne Menzies

As a teenager Anne lived in Rome, Athens, Beirut and East Africa absorbing their cultures and cuisines daily as well as learning fluent French and Italian. Later she trained in 5 star hotels like the St Georges in Beirut, the Hilton in Milan, the Royal Olympic Athens and Ashoka in New-Delhi, which at the time specialised in lavish state banquets.

She joined the leading firm of Coopers and Lybrand (now Pricewaterhouse Coopers) as a management consultant. There she carried out hotel and leisure assignments both in the UK and overseas. Later as Head of Product Development at the English Tourist Board, she wrote the book "Retail Tourism and Leisure" and many other articles for leading catering and economic journals. She led the team that created the Upper Crust food concept – still a successful brand.

It is only very recently therefore that her recipe writing career began. She formed an association with Corpus Christi College Cambridge and was privileged to research Elizabethan Cookery from original documents. She later staged a highly successful and authentic Elizabethan feast for the Guild of Benefactors in college. From there her reputation grew and she is now commissioned by a number of corporations to research and develop modern original or historic recipes for corporate entertainment.

She has a large organic vegetable and herb garden which gives her fresh produce and inspiration. Her olive oil (which won first prize in Paris this year!) and good, honest wine comes from her farm in the South of France.

Dave Reddin BSc, MSc.

After completing both an undergraduate and then a master degree in Sports Science, Dave went on to work for the Sports Council also at Loughborough University. During 7 years there he gained extensive experience in working with Elite athletes from a wide range of sports. Dave has worked as a consultant to many sports organisations including the Football Association, professional cricket and football teams, as well as the ITV network show Bodyheat.

Dave began working with England in the 1997 season following two years working at Leicester with the Tigers. After briefly working with the U21 development squad at the SANZAR tournament in 1998 he rejoined the senior squad and is now the National Fitness Advisor responsible for the physical preparation of England's top players. He is widely credited with instilling a new professional mentality into the squad having implemented detailed training and dietary programmes for all the players.

Roz Kadir RGN, Dip ION, MSc

After qualifying as a nurse at University College Hospital Roz gained extensive experience in operating theatres, coronary and intensive care units.

A love of equestrian sports took her away from the hospital environment and she subsequently ran her own stables for many years. This spawned an interest in nutrition as she questioned the diets of horses before and after competitions. This led to a progression to human nutrition and was followed by studying this subject at the Institute of Optimum Nutrition. She went onto be a lecturer and tutor at the Institute while working in the fitness industry, particularly in health clubs.

Following a chance meeting with Dr Adam Carey, she assisted him in setting up the clinic four years ago. Since then, she and her colleagues at CNM have looked after many elite athletes in team and track and field sports.

The Centre for Nutritional Medicine Ltd provide nutritional products and dietary advice to elite athletes including the England Rugby Team. Since individual dietary needs will vary, readers are advised to seek professional advice before attempting to reproduce a performance diet plan from the information in this book.
Contact: info@nutritionalmedicine.co.uk tel: 0207 907 1660. fax: 0207 907 1661.

Dave Rogers Senior Rugby Photographer for Allsport
Dave Rogers began covering sports events in 1975 and photographed his first rugby international, Ireland v Scotland, in 1978. Since then he estimates photographing over 300 rugby internationals but has lost count! He has also covered three Olympic Games, three Soccer World Cups, five Ryder Cups, six Lions Tours and every Rugby World Cup.

Dave was born in the West Midlands and now lives in Northampton and has worked for Allsport since 1993. Allsport is owned by Getty Images, the largest sports picture agency in the world.

Tony Harris Photographer - Food
Tony's association with food, (subject rather than pleasure), started in the early 80s. 'Start Living Now' was his first book with an early emphasis on whole food and exercise.

Later, his contribution helped the London Hilton on Park Lane win the global 'Maurice Raymondo Award' for Excellence in Food and Beverage. He went on to produce photographic wine lists, cocktail cards, etc. for a number of Hiltons.

Some of the food briefs in the early 90's were quite bizarre and included a double page spread, lobster and salmon mirroring a design of red and silver shoes followed by an explosion of eastern promise for the launch of the Tokyo FT.

Back to food & hotels again, 'Plums on the bed' for St Ermin's, and 'Figs & flowers for breakfast' at Thistle, 'Strawberries on the jacuzzi' at Pennyhill Park. Now that the look is 'lifestyle' food is more approachable never a problem for Tony's waistline!

Tony has a particular empathy with this project as, five years ago, his son was paralysed for many harrowing weeks by a virus.

You can contact Tony Harris at his London studio on 020 7385 8158 or email tony@TonyHphoto.com

James Senior Designer
James was born and raised in Yorkshire. After rejecting advice from school masters to "take up banking and keep art as a hobby", he went on to gain a reputation as a much respected and highly talented multi-disciplinary designer. James pursued his passion for art to the famous Jacob Kramer College of Art in Leeds. He studied graphic design at North Staffordshire Polytechnic becoming one of the few students to sucessfully gain employment before graduating. In London, James worked for a number of advertising and design companies and went on to own, manage and direct his own top 100 design consultancy. He now works as an independent design consultant specialising in corporate identity and corporate literature.
js@jamessenior.net

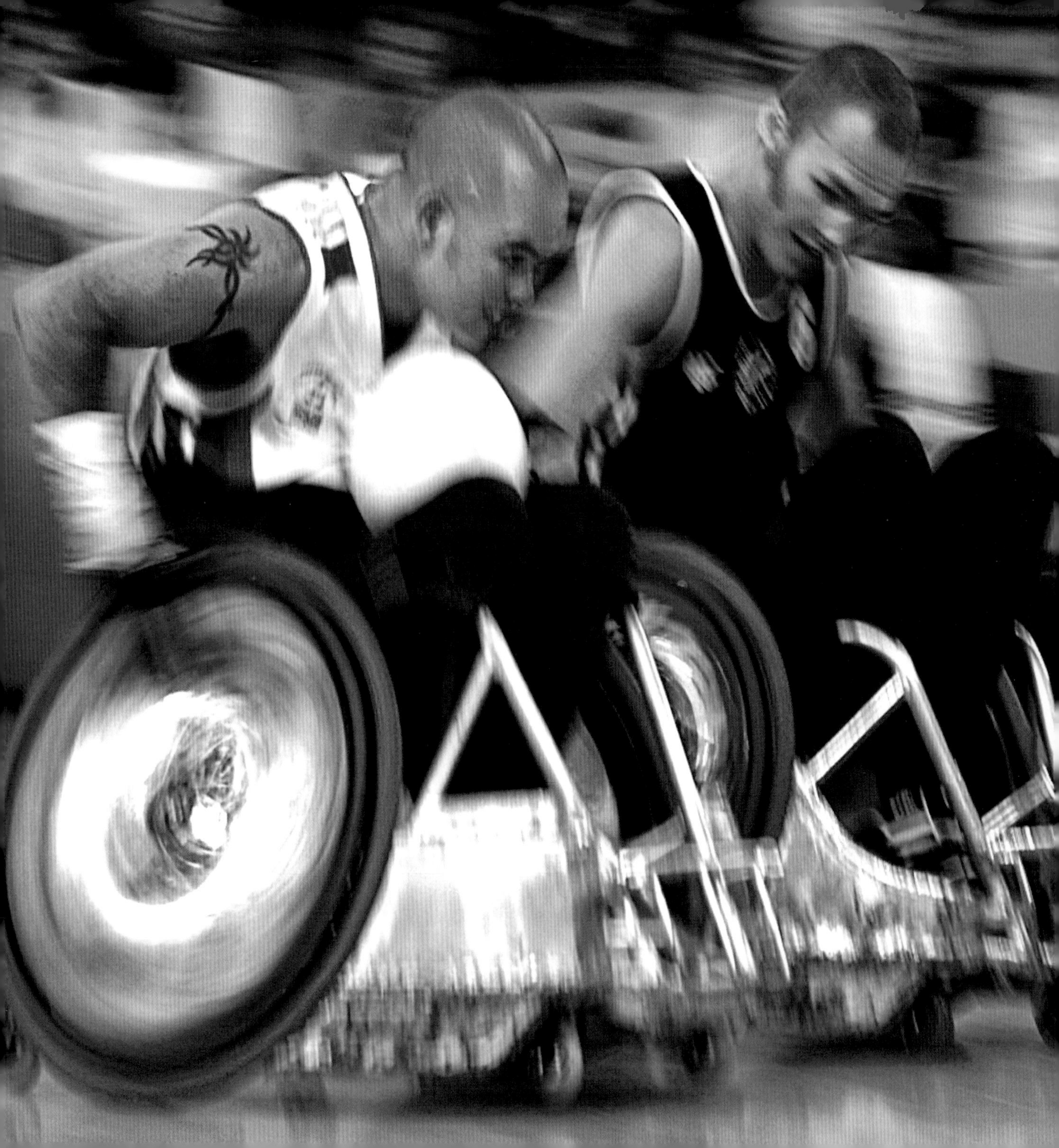

The England rugby team has been the most wonderful supporter of The Sporting Chance Appeal over the last three years. Clive Woodward, his coaching team and all the players have been so generous with their time and support and have managed to raise over £300,000 for their fellow athletes, who train and compete at our national wheelchair sports centre at Stoke Mandeville.

At Stoke Mandeville we passionately believe that people with any disability should be given the chance to take part in sport within the same professional surroundings as the best of our able bodied sportsmen. Our centre at Stoke Mandeville was the birthplace of the Paralympic Games and is recognised throughout the world as "the home of wheelchair sport". Our problem is that it is in a desperate state of disrepair and we have therefore been forced to undertake a £9.5 million rebuilding and refurbishment programme so that all our disabled sportsmen, women and children can also have their sporting chance.

All proceeds of this book go to the Sporting Chance Appeal and we are indebted to Jayne Woodward for turning Clive's idea into reality and for pulling together such a team of professionals to do it for her. Not one of them has charged a fee for their hours and days of work, so a huge thank you to Anne Menzies for her recipes and her writing, to Dave Reddin and Roz Kadir for their massive nutritional input and to Dave Rogers and Tony Harris for their stunning photography. Many thanks also to Libby Willis for her painstaking editing and to Paul Vaughan and the RFU and everyone at Twickenham and their team training HQ at Pennyhill Park. Finally a big thank you to Jim Senior, our designer, who has devoted so much of his time to turn all this work into the wonderful book that you now see.

We hope that you have a lot of fun from this book and will enjoy a healthier lifestyle by savouring the results of some of these recipes. We can assure you that thousands of people with disabilities will get lasting enjoyment from their involvement in sport at all levels thanks in part to your support.

The Sporting Chance Appeal
In aid of The British Wheelchair Sports Foundation
Registered Charity no: 265498
Telephone: 01296 395995

"England are arguably the fittest and most powerful team in world rugby today. This is the result of their dedication to fitness and nutrition - the driving force behind this book"
Clive Woodward
"At last, a recipe book of healthy, nutritious food that my whole family and I can enjoy"
Lawrence Dallaglio
"All the recipes in this book are simple to follow, take no time to prepare and actually do you good"
Martin Johnson
"Rugby's culture has changed in an unbelievable way. These days, England's players have changed shape, gaining power and athleticism from the latest theories of conditioning and nutrition. Farewell, the pie and the pint!"
Stephen Jones, Sunday Times
The Sporting Chance Appeal, FREEPOST SC 9476 Stoke Mandeville HP21 9BR England
£14.99